Stories of Biblical Mothers

Maternal Power in the Hebrew Bible

Leila Leah Bronner

UNIVERSITY PRESS OF AMERICA,® INC.
Dallas • Lanham • Boulder • New York • Oxford

Copyright © 2004 by
University Press of America,® Inc.
4501 Forbes Boulevard
Suite 200
Lanham, Maryland 20706
UPA Acquisitions Department (301) 459-3366

PO Box 317
Oxford
OX2 9RU, UK

All rights reserved
Printed in the United States of America
British Library Cataloging in Publication Information Available

Library of Congress Control Number: 2004102469
ISBN 0-7618-2828-1 (clothbound : alk. ppr.)
ISBN 0-7618-2829-X (paperback : alk. ppr.)

∞™ The paper used in this publication meets the minimum
requirements of American National Standard for Information
Sciences—Permanence of Paper for Printed Library Materials,
ANSI Z39.48—1992

For My Mother,
Rebbetzin Rachel Amsel

*"Many women have done valiantly,
But you have surpassed them all."*
Proverbs 31:29

Contents

Preface		vii
Introduction		ix
1	The First Mothers	1
2	Mothers of a Budding Nation	26
3	Wise Women and Queen Mothers	42
4	Mothers and Daughters	59
5	Metaphorical Mothers	78
6	Unconventional Mothers	95
7	The Motherly Role of God	106
Conclusion		119
Bibliography		123
Index		135
Index of Scriptural References		141

Preface

This project began, as so many do, with a small seed of an idea, which gradually blossomed into a full-fledged study. I noticed as I read through the Bible, that despite the androcentric character of the text, there are a surprising number of stories that factor in strong women. As I further studied these accounts, I noticed that many of these women found their strength in being mothers! I concluded that biblical mothers seemed to enjoy a certain measure of power, and at times were able to exert great influence within the familial and social realm. This observation led me to do a study involving the mothers of the Bible in order to see if this phenomenon of female power played itself out in all the genres of biblical literature. Thankfully, my research was not in vain; I found that the biblical mother does have recognizable power, participating in many facets of life.

During my study, I investigated a series of questions: How do mothers acquire power? What is the nature of their power? How is their influence felt in the home and within larger society? Is maternal power recognized within the Bible itself? Has this motherly influence impacted the role mothers play in later times? Some of these queries were answered by my work; others invite further reflection.

Many of the ideas expounded upon in this book had already been developed to some extent in prior articles I had written. I presented some of these articles at several conferences of the American Academy of Religion, Society of Biblical Literature, and at the World Congress of Jewish Studies in Jerusalem. Many of these ideas were further elaborated on in various lectures I gave to a variety of audiences in Los Angeles, New York, and Jerusalem. Chapter 7, "The Motherly Role of God," appeared as "Gynomorphic Imagery in the Bible" in the *Jewish Bible Quarterly*, formerly called *Dor Le Dor*. Portions of

Chapter 4, "Mothers and Daughters," appeared as "The Invisible Relationship Made Visible: Biblical Mothers and Daughters" in *Ruth and Esther: A Feminist Companion to the Bible*, edited by Athalya Brenner. As the research has progressed, my ideas have evolved and taken on new shape. Consequently, the above-mentioned chapters as they appear in this book have all been thoroughly reworked and reedited. All the other material has been composed with the topic at hand in mind and specifically for this book.

Passages quoted from the Hebrew Bible reflect my consultation of a variety of translations that I then combined into my own more readable rendition. I have relied on the general, rather than scientific transliteration of Hebrew words in order to make the work more accessible to those who do not read Hebrew. These transliterations follow the *Encyclopedia Judaica*. Translations from the Mishna, Babylonian Talmud, and *Midrash Rabba*, have been taken from the Soncino editions. Occasionally, I have altered translations to make them smoother and more readable. Abbreviations of the names of Talmudic tractates and most midrashim follow the simplified system of the *Encyclopedia Judaica*.

Among the many scholars, friends and colleagues who have assisted me, I am especially indebted to Tal Ilan, Lecturer at the Rothberg School for Overseas Students at the Hebrew University in Jerusalem, who read the preliminary manuscript and made many valuable suggestions. Angela Bauer, Professor of Bible at the Episcopal Divinity School in Cambridge, Massachusetts, also deserves recognition for her patient reading and rereading of the manuscript. She made helpful comments regarding the overriding theme and arrangement of the chapters of the book. I also want to acknowledge Shulamit Valler, Lecturer of Talmud at Haifa University with whom I had many stimulating conversations about the role and place of women within Jewish tradition. This present study profited much from the assistance of David Hirsch, Jewish Studies Bibliographer of the Young Research Library of UCLA, who aided me in obtaining useful study material. I also benefited from the rich resources of the Frances Henry Library of Hebrew Union College, Los Angeles campus, through the ready assistance of Yaffa Weisman, Director.

Special appreciation is due to Alicia Magal, for her devoted and dedicated assistance in researching, editing and typing the manuscript. I also acknowledge Amy Sapowith, who aided with the work. Cara Swanson, Ph.D candidate in Near Eastern Languages and Cultures at UCLA, has been accommodating in patiently researching, editing and helping shape the final form of this manuscript. To all who have helped in the culmination of this work, I offer many thanks. Responsibility for the book, both what it contains and what it lacks, is of course, my own.

Introduction

The mother of the Bible is a figure of power. She influences the course of life in her home and, in some cases, wider society. The biblical mother is a force to be reckoned with in social, political and religious spheres. Her power stems in part from her role as wife, but far more so from the nurturing and influential relationship she has with her children. No other biblical woman, whether wife, sister or daughter, seems to enjoy the same status and power as the mother. As the mother of the Bible cares for her clan, she does so with wisdom and purpose, acquiring authority and position within the household and beyond.

Some feminists assert that a biblical woman's function is to fulfill and sanction the demands of patriarchy. However, as a feminist and biblical scholar I maintain that women as mothers are not merely constructed as male-dependent pawns within the biblical narrative. Though they are confined to the parameters of a patriarchal system, they have room to operate within their own initiative. They accomplish real feats and emerge as memorable biblical figures, as I demonstrate.

What type of power did a mother enjoy in the ancient biblical world? Here we must turn our attention to anthropologists who have commented on the topic of social power. Anthropologists differentiate between "authority," which denotes culturally sanctioned hierarchical control, and "power," which is described as the ability to gain compliance from others. While generally speaking women did not find themselves in a position where they could claim legal "authority," they certainly had access to "unassigned power," that is, unofficial influence and persuasion.[1] They used unorthodox methods to obtain their desired end since women could not acquire power through conventional means. Their strategies of persuasion and manipulation are a response to the unequal distribution of power and authority in society. A mother often used her ingenuity to influence people around her because she was not granted official authority by society. She challenged her cultural, social, political and religious environment and made a livable reality for herself.

The unofficial power women exercised has largely gone unnoticed, due to limitations within the historical records. With few exceptions, women did not feature prominently in the history of any civilization.[2] History has traditionally recorded the achievements and trials of the powerful elite, while the institutions that affect individuals on the social level, such as marriage and family, have remained, until recent times, outside the scope of historical inquiry.[3] Indeed, it has been asserted that "social history deals with the banal; historical sources prefer the extraordinary."[4] Because the vast majority of women were conditioned and limited to marriage, motherhood and home, their talents in other spheres remained largely untapped, underdeveloped and unrecorded. However, the Bible is not altogether silent regarding the importance of women. What the Bible chooses to record about the mothers of ancient Israel deserves close attention.

At no time were biblical women entirely dominated and disempowered by a society that restricted a woman's legal and public opportunities. As Otwell argues, not only were women held in high regard in ancient Israel, they were not totally relegated, as some have assumed, to an inferior position within the ancient patriarchal system.[5] In other words, they were able to acquire some measure of power and status. I argue that this was particularly true in their role as mother. As we will discuss below, sometimes mothers of the Bible found power as queen mothers and wise women, caring for and counseling their families and their people.

Feminist scholars have traditionally been bothered by the male-centered tone of the Bible, and studies conducted over the past thirty years have served as correctives to these patriarchal assumptions.[6] But these feministic analyses are in no way homogenous. Their scope and breadth runs the gamut. Some studies emphasize the patriarchal tone of the Bible and see little positive female figures emerge. Other studies downplay the androcentric nature of the Bible and reclaim the female figure as a model of great significance. My study, acknowledging the patriarchal character of the Hebrew Bible, analyzes the role of the mother within the admittedly limited environment in which she functioned. While some scholars project upon the text a certain agenda on the part of the male writers to limit the power women held in society,[7] I choose instead to describe the unassigned power of the mother in the literary world of the Bible. I claim that women as mothers emerge as paragons of power, figures of faith, and archetypes of ingenuity.

To my knowledge, no comprehensive book has dealt with the topic of motherhood in the Bible. Although many articles exist, they usually comprise a chapter in a larger study that talks about the place of women within the biblical landscape. My analysis of the biblical mother shows that women had power in the context of their mothering. I appreciate Frymer-Kensky's question, "Why are there so many memorable women in the Bible [in this androcentric text]?"[8] I attempt to provide an answer to this question by analyzing the unforgettable mothers of the biblical narrative. I look at prominent figures but also deal with lesser-known characters. My study includes both named and unnamed mothers within the Bible. My investigation goes from Eve to Esther, Rahab to Ruth, Bathsheba to Nahushta, and includes many other maternal figures. I show that all these mothers are unique in personality and behavior and manage to impact their respective homes and communities, yet at the same time are connected in that they all rely on skillfully acquired, yet unassigned power.

When one begins to consider mothering, one often begins with marriage, a strong social tie within a complex kinship system that entails the merging of two or more families and possibly two or more traditions.[9] To tap into any potential power, a woman must transition from daughter to wife to mother. Becoming a wife is the usual prelude to becoming a mother of future children. For this reason alone the woman who is taken as a wife is empowered by the importance of her eventual role; she is the progenitress of the future, bringing with her a set of beliefs and customs to impart to her children. As Frymer-Kensky notes, a wife/mother goes from being "outside the family into its very heart as the bearer and caretaker of its future children."[10] Through the institution of marriage a comparatively powerless daughter rises to the respected stature accorded a mother. This is the kind of unofficial power referred to above, in the familial relationships of the Bible where a mother figures prominently. A woman in her lifetime, may go from the position of vulnerable daughter to the position of wife, and finally, reach the most powerful position, that of Influential Mother.

The book contains seven chapters, with an introduction and conclusion. These chapters chronologically deal with a wide range of mothers in their different familial relationships and settings. Each individual has her own outlook on life, style of mothering, and degree of piety. The theme of motherly influence governs our agenda and we examine different aspects of the overriding premise in each of the chapters of the book.

Chapter One, "The First Mothers," deals with the ancient mothers and foundational matriarchs of Genesis, who live in a close-knit clan society. These mothers exercise their influence within a familial setting. This chapter mines the biblical text for the intimacy displayed between the various mothers and their sons. Because these relationships exist more between the lines than explicitly stated in the text, I discover intimations of relationship from the characters' names, which often in the Bible shed light on an individual's personality and behavior. In the Genesis stories, the presence of God and the themes of covenant and faith inform the beliefs, actions and longings of these early matriarchs. They are nurturing a family that is on the brink of becoming a people.

Chapter Two, "Mothers of a Budding Nation," notes the different relationships between mothers and sons found in the books of Judges, Samuel and Kings as compared to those found in first five books of the Bible. These mothers are living during an age of transition. They are nurturing sons who go on to contribute to the birth of a nation. In contrast to the view of motherhood in the Pentateuch, the mothers of these later books exhibit a broader range of maternal attitudes. Although women like Hannah echo the Genesis matriarchs desire for children, other women, such as Samson's mother and the Shunammite, do not yearn desperately to give birth.

Chapter Three, "Wise Women and Queen Mothers," explores how some women experience their motherhood more in terms of nurturing a nation than raising a child. In these examples of wise women and queen mothers, motherhood extends its influence beyond the immediate family into the halls of wisdom and the corridors of royalty. The mothering these women do has far-reaching impact in that they often influence a whole people group by their actions. They employ motherly concern and intuition to bring about social, political and religious change.

Chapter Four, "Mothers and Daughters," addresses first the metaphor of the daughter of Israel used throughout the Hebrew Bible to express the relationship between God and his people. Then the chapter delves into the personal and domestic realm of mothers and their daughters. The Bible relates only three stories that feature a daughter whose mother's name is specified. I have added to these stories the example of Rebecca and her mother in addition to examples from Ruth and the Song of Songs where the central relationship can be identified as one between a mother and daughter. These stories show another dimension to the topic of motherhood. Though the Bible is replete with mother-son accounts, the little information on the interaction between mother and daughter often goes unnoticed. However, these important relationships show that biblical women can empower one another to be strong in the face of great hardship.

Chapter Five, "The Metaphorical Mother," delves into a new area of study, exploring the exceptional role a few notable women play as large scale leaders. They are not biological mothers, but become symbolic mothers through their outstanding devotion to their people. The chapter begins with a discussion of Deborah and offers her as an important paradigm for other women leaders of the Bible who can be characterized as "mothers in Israel." These women are unique in social standing and behavior. Their "mothering" becomes a style of leadership, which differs significantly from how their male colleagues govern their people.

Chapter Six, "The Unconventional Mother," looks at women who become mothers through unusual means. We study the "daughters of men" of Genesis 6 who mate with divine beings and give birth to demigods. We also examine Lot's daughters who procreate with their father to give birth to the eponymous ancestors of the Moabites and Ammonites. Finally, we investigate the unorthodox coupling of Tamar with her father-in-law, Judah. The unconventional method these women use to conceive deserves explanation and commentary.

Chapter Seven, entitled "The Motherly Role of God," portrays the aspect of God that mirrors the tasks and activities typically attributed to the mother. That the biblical writers utilized female, and particularly maternal images for God I believe shows that the role of the mother was held in high esteem. The Hebrew Bible rejects the idea of God as either exclusively male or female. According to this theology, God the Creator transcends both sexes. In this chapter I focus on the nurturing and maternal imagery describing God's interaction with his people.

METHODOLOGY

My study is a literary one in which I engage in narrative criticism, examining each biblical periscope to determine the role the mother plays. I consider the mother stories as a group, thematically studying each in reference to the other, analyzing their composition and purpose, in an attempt to give as comprehensive view as possible of the biblical mother. Every mother story differs in context and situation. In doing a wide-ranging study of most of the mothers of the Bible, I show that biblical women are remarkable, and make valuable contributions within their respective communities. They transform themselves, their children, and often their entire social world.

As I mention above, this study employs first and foremost literary criticism. Literary criticism, or narrative criticism, analyzes the features that the narrator uses to develop not only an individual narrative, but also to deliberately link it with other stories in the larger context for distinctive design. In order to bring out the subtle nuances of the literary record, I compare and contrast how various characters interact and behave. Instead of focusing on the patchwork of documents scholars have recognized as the Bible, I emphasize the final form of the text. My approach uses the canonical shape of the Bible as a starting point, thus I study each mother chronologically, as presented, with the few exceptions noted.

This book aims to offer a new appreciation for the mothers of the Bible. For the most part I discuss biological mothers, but the study also includes women in the Bible who act in a mothering capacity by caring for symbolic children. These women, although not mothers on a physical level, appear as mothers on a metaphorical, or symbolic level. In studying the mothers of the Bible, I seek to recognize the extraordinary in the ordinary. The mother is a powerful force within the family, and indirectly her influence resonates at times within the public domain. On the other hand, at some crucial moments, we do not hear the mother's voice. We can only speculate at the dialogue that might have occurred within the family behind closed doors, which might have led to actions taken on the part of the husband or brothers. The objective in my research is neither to extol nor to denigrate, but to make the implicit in the text explicit.

My research begins by studying the original languages, as I believe that examining the Hebrew and Aramaic offers a major clue to interpreting the women of this tradition. I employ a literary critical technique of close reading to examine grammar, syntax and etymology and to interpret linguistic connections. I also, when possible give a translation for a character's name, often relying on the popular meaning rather than strict linguistic interpretation in an attempt to offer a new dimension to this study. At the same time, I do not hesitate to supplement the biblical stories with related historical and social phenomena in an interdisciplinary analysis of what these biblical texts may mean to us. I draw both from traditional Jewish sources, such as the Talmud and Midrash, and contemporary critical analysis to situate my investigation within the parameters of rabbinic tradition and modern biblical studies. Since my interest is the final form of the text, I do not distinguish documentary sources nor discuss in detail problems of authorship. I cull from various versions, consult many, and in the final analysis, many of the biblical translations are my own.

This inquiry on biblical motherhood was undertaken because of my desire to study a little-explored topic. I hope through this study to bring to the forefront an overlooked figure in the Hebrew Bible. In doing a wide-ranging study of most of the mothers of the Bible, I show that these biblical women are remarkable figures of fortitude, and make valuable contributions within their communities. Indeed these amazing women continue to wield influence today in the on-going analysis of the literary testimony of their lives. The ancestral mothers of Israel truly are extraordinary women. Through their example we are encouraged to be stronger, wiser, more assertive, more courageous, in short, proactive in our posture toward life.

NOTES

1. Michelle Z. Rosaldo and Louise Lamphere, eds., *Woman, Culture & Society* (Stanford, California: Stanford University Press, 1974), 99

2. Myra N.Shoub, "Jewish Women's History: Development of a Critical Methodology," *Conservative Judaism*, Vol.XXXV, no.2, (Winter 1982): 33 ff. ; for other feminist points of view, please see N. Aschkenasy, "A Non-Sexist Reading of the Bible," *Midstream*, Vol. XXVII, no. 6 (June/July 1981): 51–55. Mary Daly, *Beyond God the Father* (Boston: Beacon Press, 1973); Rosemary Radford Reuther, *Religion and Sexism* (New York, New York: Simon and Schuster, 1974),99.

3. Myra N. Shoub, "Jewish Women's History: Development of a Critical Methodology," *Conservative Judaism*, Vol. XXXV, no. 2, (Winter 1982): 33 ff. and Bibliography mentioned in this article.

4. Tal Ilan, *Jewish Women in Greco-Roman Palestine*, (Peabody, MA: Hendrickson, 1996), 42; *Integrating Women into Second Temple History* (Hendrickson, Peabody, MA, 2001), 1. She writes; "History (all history, including Jewish history) looks devoid of women."

5. See study on women by John H. Otwell, *And Sarah Laughed* (Philadelphia, Westminster Press, 1977), 1–13.

6. Cheryl Exum, *Fragmented Women* (Valley Forge: Trinity Press International, 1993); Esther Fuchs, *Sexual Politics in the Biblical Narrative* (Sheffield Academic Pres, 2000); For others, see Bibliography.

7. Esther Fuchs, "The Literary Characterizaion of Mothers and Sexual Politics in the Hebrew Bible," in *Semeia* 46 (1989): 151–166

8. Tikvah Frymer-Kensky, *Reading the Women of the Bible* (New York: Schocken Books, 2002), xv.

9. We are aware that some biblical women become mothers outside the institution of marriage. Some came into motherhood as harlots, concubines, and maidservants. In Chapter 5 we discuss "Metaphorical Mothers, who may or who may not be married (and who may or may not have biological children) In Chapter 6 we deal with "Unconventional Mothers" who do not go through the usual channels of social progression from marriage to motherhood. As they arise, we also address the handmaids of the matriarchs, who also do not "marry" in the usual sense.

10. Frymer-Kensky, 335.

Chapter One

The First Mothers

> *. . . . she was the mother of all the living.*
>
> Genesis 3:20b

> *Men are what their mothers make them.*
>
> EMERSON, *Conduct of Life: Fate*

The book of Genesis is a book of beginnings: the beginning of the world, the beginning of Israel, and the beginning of the foremothers and forefathers of ancient Israel. The literary record of these early mothers lays a foundation by which we read the rest of God's involvement in human history. The women of Genesis reveal that women play an important role in a patriarchal society, and poignantly show human sadness and joy, weakness and strength, failure and freedom.

We start our study with Eve, the mother of all living. Though the judgment oracle refers to the pain she will subsequently experience in childbirth, she rejoices at the arrival of a new son. She is a strong mother, a woman who boldly announces that she (with the help of God) has created a child. Our study then focuses on the early matriarchal figure, Sarah, who the text presents as a woman of great beauty and courage in the face of much hardship. We then move on to discuss the experiences of the other matriarchs, who each in her own way challenges the social order and overcomes adversity. In our study, we see that these women, as mothers, work to direct, shape and secure the destiny of their families.

EVE

Eve, the very first woman created by God (Genesis 2:21–22), has been the topic of theological debate over a woman's role in society throughout history.[1] She appears frequently in later Jewish, Christian and Muslim sources as a temptress and an archetype of sin. Yet images of Eve's motherhood, whether fulfilled or bereft, are often overlooked, and can serve to re-conceptualize her as an archetype of motherhood. With this purpose in mind, I concentrate solely on Eve's role as mother and her somewhat limited relationship with her sons, Cain, Abel and Seth, which only is demonstrated through the naming process. As the first mother in history, Eve is an archetypal mother, and the only woman in scripture to have the text explain the meaning of her name, "She was the mother of all the living" (Gen. 3:20).

Before we launch into a discussion of Eve, we should make a comment about the issue of naming within the Bible. In the ancient world a name is a distinguishing mark which often foretells the bearer's future or reflects the namer's experience in life or hopes for the future. A name may also denote the essence of a person or place. To name is to know. As noted in the *Anchor Bible Dictionary*, "the knowledge of the name opens up specific human dimensions for communication and for fellowship."[2] When a name is known, an avenue for relationship opens up, and the given name often provides definition for the relationship. As seen in the Creation account in which Adam names all the animals (Gen.2:19, 20), naming was a way in which a power relationship is established. Adam is given authority over the creation, and his dominion is demonstrated through the act of naming. Yet, in some cases (which we will discuss at greater length below), a name defines and reveals the character of the person named, or speaks to the destiny of the one who does the naming. Significantly, twenty-seven of the namers of the Bible are mothers, while only seventeen are fathers. Mothers of the Bible predominantly are the namers of their children.

In addition to establishing relationship, names also bring definition and order. A name provides a category, and it functions in this manner with regards to Eve. Eve, "mother of all living," is so named not to reflect male power over her, but rather to express her special relationship within the newly created order. She is differentiated from male, and given a role in the new world. She is the mother of all living, a mother *par excellence*. With her begins the institution of motherhood, and she provides boundaries for all subsequent mothers. Are these boundaries positive ones? There are some scholars who would see her designation as "Eve" a way of imprisoning her within motherhood.[3] Rather than expresses imprisonment, we suggest that the text expresses Eve's joy, freedom, and even power exercised within her role as mother.

Eve describes with great excitement the wondrous process of giving birth to her son. "And she [Eve] conceived and bore Cain saying, 'I have created [gained] (*qaniti*) a man with [the cooperation of] Yahweh'" (Genesis 4:1).[4] Eve's language is remarkable; she speaks of having "created," implying pleasure, rather than having "birthed," suggesting pain. Her role as new mother emphasizes her joy, not her sorrow. Eve's attitude contrasts with how later feminists would characterize the woman's plight within her role as mother. Pain and suffering experienced through childbirth define her "ultimate value in the world."[5] Motherhood in these terms does indeed seem relegated to imprisonment. Though bearing children with pain was part of Eve's punishment received in Eden, she does not issue a complaint at the pain she experiences during pregnancy and delivery. Instead, she conveys gladness, stressing the personal pronoun "I," and boasting in her creative power.

Eve's naming speech, in which she uses the term "created," represents a compelling reversal of the earlier one made by Adam. Whereas Adam almost boasted in the woman's appearance as a product of his own flesh ("bone of my bone, flesh of my flesh"), Eve turns the tables by proclaiming that the "man" she acquired was done without the assistance of Adam. Her son was born with the help of God, not her husband. Her naming speech seems to be less of a comment about her new son, and more her response to Adam's previous boldness (Gen.2:23).[6] Nonetheless, these words of elation from the lips of the first Mother, present a striking contrast to the curse of woman's pain and sadness during childbirth pronounced by God: "In pain shall you bear children" (Gen. 3:16). Might we understand that the birth of a son is an experience of such weight and magnitude that even a divine curse pales in comparison? This primordial mother appears thrilled and powerful in her new position as the mother of a son. She almost congratulates herself on having created a life.[7] Moreover, she sets the precedent for the mother's prerogative to name her children.[8]

Through the naming of her sons, Eve rejoices in her generative powers and shows that motherhood is a privilege rather than a punishment. Her bliss is unfortunately marred later when her sons have a fatal quarrel and Cain kills his brother Abel. Although she is the mother of life, she experiences that life, like a breath, is fleeting and hovers between fulfillment and failure. The meaning of her second son's name, Abel, *hevel*, meaning "breath" or "vapor," clearly suggests the fragility of life and meaning in the face of murderous jealousy. When she has another son, she names him Seth, meaning "God has provided me with another offspring in place of Abel," for Cain had killed him (Genesis 4:26). Here Eve realizes that there are limitations to her power as Mother of Life, and gives thanks to God for replacing her dead son with Seth.[9]

In contrast to Eve's first naming speech, which dramatically inaugurated maternal name-giving by connecting it with cosmic creation, her second speech is more subdued as a result of her encounter with death. Though somewhat restrained, it is still a celebration of birth. Even in the absence of dialogue between her and her sons, one senses from Eve's own joyous behavior at the births of her sons that she develops strong, loving bonds with each of them. Unfortunately, there is no explicit evidence as to whether her sons reciprocate her loving maternal feelings.

ADAH AND ZILLAH

Adah and Zillah, the two wives of Lamech descended from Cain, are briefly mentioned in Genesis. Adah bore Jabal and Jubal, and Zillah bore Tubal-Cain and Naamah. Their presence in the Bible is limited to their distinctions as mothers and wives. Lamech was wise and taught each of his three sons a craft. They are described as founders of civilization: Jabal, the father of those that dwell in tents; Jubal, the father of all who play the lyre; Tubal-Cain, the one who forged metals to make swords, spears, javelins, and all instruments of war. Why does Lamech address his wives? Apparently he is responding to their fear of weapons-making.

> Lamech said to his wives:
> Adah and Zillah, hear my voice;
> Wives of Lamech, listen to what I say:
> I have slain a man for wounding me,
> A young man for striking me.
> If Cain is avenged sevenfold,
> Then Lamech seventy-seven fold (Gen. 4:23–24)

We speculate that his wives are afraid that he might be punished for bringing instruments of war into the world and for teaching his son the art of killing. Lamech's poetic speech is aimed at allaying their fears. His words suggest that if Cain who killed with intent had his punishment delayed for seven generations, then Lamech would be safe since his punishment would be delayed many times seven since he killed merely accidentally.[10]

The Midrash weaves interesting fantasies into the laconic story of Lamech.[11] The Midrash claims that his wives refused to have sexual relations with him as they did not want to bear children to be destroyed. "They said to him: 'Tomorrow a flood will come—are we to bear children?'" Lamech summoned them to their marital duties, explaining that he was a peaceful man and no harm would befall them and their children. Though Lamech wanted them to engage in sexual relations, they refused to comply with his desires. They were using the one thing at their means as a way of controlling their future.

Thus the passage about Adah and Zillah portrays the values of mothers early in the Bible and reinforced in the Midrash. Tradition shows that mothers were deeply devoted to their children's protection and longevity. Having given birth, they further the march of civilization and are terrified that weapons of war might destroy their offspring. As mothers they are concerned with the welfare of their sons and all future generations; like Eve, they are proponents of life, not death.

SARAH

The most well known mothers in the Bible are the matriarchs Sarah, Rebecca, Rachel and Leah. The first three require much prayer and patience before they are able to conceive. It is only Leah who is effortlessly fecund. Why is so much attention put on the barrenness of the matriarchs? What do we learn about them as mothers once they are given the gift of progeny?

The first verse describing Sarah on a genealogical list as she accompanies her husband Abraham into the Land of Canaan, informs: "Sarah was barren; she had no child" (Gen. 11:29). This focus on her childlessness prepares us for the importance this theme will play in the life story of Sarah and Abraham (Gen. 11:30). While Sarah does play a necessary and crucial role in the fulfillment of divine promise, the concern of the narrative is to stress her difficulties in bearing the promised child rather than in describing her activities and influence as a mother. If we compare Sarah's difficulty with Eve's ease of conception, we might conclude that the acts of conception and creation with direct bearing on the future chosen people always incur some obstacle. This bears itself out in the stories of Rebecca and Rachel as well. The motif of miraculous birth is pivotal to the patriarchal and matriarchal narratives. If God gives a divine promise of progeny it must eventually be fulfilled.

Sarah's difficulty and desire to produce a son is so great that she offers her handmaiden Hagar to her husband as a surrogate.[12] This solution however, leads to strife between the two women.[13] Feeling provoked, Sarah impels Hagar to flee (Gen. 16:6–16). Hagar does return, and Abraham's first son, Ishmael, is born.

Eventually, three angels announce the promise of a child to Sarah. At the advanced age of ninety, Sarah gives birth to a child whom Abraham names Isaac (Yitzhak), reflecting the laughter caused by the unlikely prospect of his birth (Gen. 21:1). "Who would have said to Abraham that Sarah would suckle children, yet I have borne a son in his old age" (Gen 21:7). Interestingly, although the text does not have Sarah giving Isaac his name, she provides the justification. Again his name reflects, not his character or destiny, but rather speaks to Sarah's maternal attitude. Although she mocked the notion earlier, she rejoices with laughter at giving birth later. Further, she recognizes that others in subsequent generations will share in her joy. She seems to intuit that her role as mother will be long remembered, and contribute largely to the narrative heritage of her people. Although we are privy to very few insights regarding Sarah as a mother here we imagine her no longer hurt and forlorn at her long standing barrenness, but redeemed, relieved, grateful, and finally fulfilled.

We expect that Sarah, now a gratified mother, would develop a certain camaraderie and compassion toward Hagar, another mother. But in fact the opposite proves true. Although both women inhabited the same cultural milieu, living in a society which highly valued a woman's ability to conceive, they develop feelings of animosity toward one another. Their social environment was a breeding ground for competition between women, each vying to give birth to children. Each woman's vastly differing social class was another point to strife. One was a privileged lady, the other a lowly maidservant. When the maidservant becomes pregnant and gives birth to a son, she becomes arrogant and ungrateful, taunting Sarah's barrenness. Her ability to conceive gave her room to lord over a social superior. This behavior is not limited to biblical text; we also find examples in other Near Eastern literature.[14]

The biblical text gives it own commentary on the tension between the two women. Sarah spies Ishmael "playing," and becomes enraged. "Sarah saw the son whom Hagar the Egyptian had borne to Abraham, playing" (Gen. 21:9) and wants to banish both the maidservant and her son. The ambiguity of the biblical text leads us to question what exactly is meant by Ishmael's "playing" (*mezachek*). Clearly, the use of the term is a wordplay on Isaac's name,[15] and indeed, in other passages involving Isaac the text makes use of the same term, *mezachek*. In other places in the Bible, the verb *mezachek* has sexual connotations (Gen. 19:14, 21:9, 26:8; Ex. 32:6). Rabbinic literature offers three interpretations of *mezachek:* immorality, idolatry and bloodshed, each portraying Ishmael in a pejorative light. The Midrash bolsters this interpretation by quoting the relevant biblical verses cited above.[16] The most common interpretation of this same scene is that Sarah suddenly realizes that Ishmael is a potential rival to Isaac's patrimony and, fiercely protective of his inheritance rights, demands that he and his mother be sent away. However, we should emphasize along with this interpretation the possibility that *mezachek* had a religious connotation, and thus Sarah banished mother and child because she feared the negative cultural and religious influence Ishmael may have had on Isaac.[17]

The book of Jubilees takes a more positive approach to Ishmael, commenting that Abraham delighted in *both* his sons. Sarah then emerges as a protective mother, jealously guarding her son's rights (Jub.17:4). Another interpretation is that Sarah is apparently so morally outraged by the behavior of Ishmael that she demands from Abraham that he drive both mother and child out. Sarah disapproved of Ishmael's "playing," and worried that his untoward behavior would adversely influence Isaac. Abraham is reluctant to acquiesce to Sarah's request until God tells him to listen to his wife and fulfill her demand. God assures him that Ishmael too will be a father of a great nation (Gen. 21:11–21). Sarah receives mixed responses from traditional and contemporary biblical commentators for her banishment of Hagar. Yet remarkably, God defends Sarah: "All that Sarah says unto you, do as she says. It is through Isaac that your offspring will be carried on" (21:12). My own reading of the event is that the deity supported the promise God made to Abraham regarding Isaac. Perhaps God also felt compassion for Sarah, an old, once barren woman, who had been humiliated by a younger upstart. The tension between Sarah and Hagar will remain a vexing and unresolved problem for future exegetes of the text. This passage shows that when a mother feels her offspring is threatened, she will even attack another mother.

Rabbinic tradition regards Sarah as a venerable figure of the Bible. Abraham highly values Sarah's voice and consulted with her on many important occasions. We wonder, then, why Sarah, clearly a devoted and vigilant mother, was not consulted by her husband at the pivotal moment of Abraham's great test, the binding of Isaac? How is it possible that she was absent when her son was taken by his father Abraham to be bound for sacrifice on Mt. Moriah? Rabbinic sources grapple with this problem.

One midrash describes Abraham as vacillating over whether to tell Sarah of his intentions to comply with God's command to sacrifice their son. He tells her he is taking Isaac to study, and Sarah advises him to take him in peace. Probably the midrash wants to say, and contemporary thinking might agree, that the real reason for concealing the Akedah from Sarah was Abraham's fear that Sarah's maternal love would overpower her religious responsibility.[18] Sarah's earlier protectiveness over Isaac in the Ishmael episode would surely have continued had she known of Abraham's intention to sacrifice their son.

Another midrash describes Satan in an attempt to corrupt God's subjects and to undermine God's plan. Disguised as an old man, Satan informs Sarah that Abraham is taking their son to sacrifice him. As in the midrash above, Satan wagers that Sarah's love for her son would outweigh her duty to God.

> The Satan being annoyed that he could not frustrate God's plan concerning the sacrifice of Isaac . . . turned his attention to Sarah. He said to her, 'Your old husband

has seized the boy, and sacrificed him. The boy wailed and wept but could not escape from his father. Sarah began to cry bitterly and ultimately died of her grief.[19]

These two midrashim are based on the apposition in the text of the Akedah followed immediately by the verse announcing Sarah's death. Interestingly, the rabbis make something of the juxtaposition of the Akedah and Sarah's subsequent demise. They attribute Sarah's death to her heart-breaking sorrow after hearing of Abraham's previous intention to sacrifice their son.

Although not many modern commentators address Sarah's absence at the Akedah, we should mention one interesting interpretation here.[20] Phillis Trible criticizes the strong androcentric nature of the Akedah, claiming that "patriarchy has denied Sarah her story, the opportunity for freedom and blessing." In Trible's view, Sarah more rightly should have been tested, not Abraham, as Isaac is truly her only son. This highly original analysis, in my opinion, is perhaps over-exaggerated, but I do believe that Sarah should have been included in the decision and experience of the sacrifice. Trible's emphasis on the mother's attachment to her son is insightful and noteworthy.

The last reference to Sarah in Genesis occurs in the context of Isaac's marriage. It is important to point out that the Genesis text emphasizes Isaac's yearning for his mother after her death. "He brought Rebecca into his mother Sarah's tent, and took Rebecca, and she became his wife and he loved her: and Isaac was comforted after his mother's death" (Gen. 24:67). This sensitive verse indicates that the son reciprocated his mother's devotion and that the two of them were quite dear to one another. This is the one place in the narrative where the son's feelings for his mother are made explicit. We are to understand that in bringing a beloved wife into his mother's tent, Isaac transfers the deep love he had felt for his mother, Sarah, to his spouse, Rebecca. The rabbis develop this approach as well.[21] Though modern psychology finds disturbing a son forming a strong attachment to his mother, the rabbis see a beauty in the strong filial relationship between mother and son.

The name "Sarah" is usually explained as "princess" derived from the root *s-r-r*, meaning "to rule."[22] But her name connotes something more than ladyship if the spelling of Sarah is derived from a second Hebrew root, *s-r-h*. This root means according to Jacob's encounter with the angel "to strive with God and man and to prevail" (Gen. 32:29). If we assume her character more closely conforms to the second root, *s-r-h*, then her name would suggest a person great strength of will who struggled against societal constraints. She opposed Abraham by demanding the expulsion of the maid who scorned her. Both of the roots, *s-r-r* and *s-r-h* contain within them the idea of persistence. Does this shared root connection signify a special relationship between Sarah the matriarch and her grandson Jacob (Israel)? Perhaps the text wishes to show that both parties struggled with difficult relationships, both with God and with humans. Like Jacob, Sarah eventually is able to rise above her circumstances and overcome some of life's hardships. Sarah struggled with her husband, Abraham, and she struggled with the harsh conditions of her time, and ultimately she prevailed.

What does Sarah teach us about motherhood? What do we learn from the example of her life? She endured a long period of shameful barrenness with some forbearance. However, her ordeal with a much younger rival wife who taunted her infertility moved Sarah to take action against Hagar. And perhaps here in our final note we should mention that although Sarah had lived assertively for the bulk of her life as a dominant and barren matriarch, she most strongly emerges as a distinct voice in the biblical text during situations relating to her fertility and subsequent motherhood.

HAGAR

Hagar's story provides an interesting foil to the stories of the matriarchs. Though she is a mere servant, she is only the woman in Genesis who experiences multiple theophanies. Unlike many of the other women of Genesis she does not struggle with barrenness or experience any trouble in conceiving. However, her encounter with motherhood, though seemingly welcome, almost instantly brings turmoil and strife.

The tension between Sarah and Hagar is well-known. One is old and barren, the other, young and fertile. One is the lady of the house, the other, a lowly maidservant. Hagar's pregnancy (and perhaps her growing attachment to Abraham?), leads Sarah to oppress her maidservant. The word used in the text for "oppress" suggests physical and psychological abuse. The text does not spell out what Sarah did, but whatever the nature of the oppression, Hagar was moved to leave, and fled into the wilderness.

> An angel of the LORD found her by a spring of water in the wilderness, the spring on the road to Shur, and said, "Hagar, slave of Sarai, where have you come from, and where are you going?" And she said, "I am running away from my mistress Sarai." And the angel of the LORD said to her, "Go back to your mistress, and submit to her harsh treatment." And the angel of the LORD said to her, "I will greatly increase your offspring, and they shall be too many to count." The angel of the LORD said to her further, "Behold, you are with child and you shall bear a son; You shall call him Ishmael, for the Lord has paid heed to your suffering." . . . And she called the LORD who spoke to her, "You are El-roi," by which she meant, "Have I not seen him who has seen me!" . . . Hagar bore a son to Abram, and Abram gave that son that Hagar bore him the name Ishmael. (16:7–15)

Hagar's life changes dramatically when Sarah eventually does conceive. Up until that point, we assume Hagar had lived securely in Abraham's household as co-wife along with Sarah.[23] Hagar's two episodes in the wilderness are strikingly different. The first theophany occurred after Sarah's treatment of Hagar, the second occurs after Ishmael's treatment of Isaac. One almost gets the sense that the son is making up for the poor treatment his mother, the lowly maidservant, had received under her mistress.

When Hagar is expelled (Genesis 21:15), the suffering of the mother and child exemplifies Hagar's devotion to Ishmael. "When the water was gone from the skin, she left the child under one of the bushes, and went and sat down at a distance, a bowshot away; for she thought, 'Let me not look on as the child dies.' And sitting thus afar, she burst into tears" (Gen. 21:16). Then the text amplifies upon God's response to the mother and son:

> And she wandered about in the wilderness of Beer-sheba. When the water was gone from the skin, she left the child under one of the bushes, and went and sat down at a distance, a bowshot away; for she thought, "Let me not look on as the child dies." And sitting thus afar, she burst into tears. God hears the cry of the boy, and an angel of God called to Hagar from heaven and said to her, "What troubles you, Hagar? Fear not, for God has heeded the cry of the boy where he is. Come, lift up the boy and hold him by the hand, for I will make a great nation of him." Then God opened her eyes and she saw a well of water. . . . God was with the boy and he grew up; he dwelt in the wilderness and became a bowman. He lived in the wilderness of Paran; and his mother got a wife for him from the land of Egypt (Genesis 14b-21).

Strangely, the text first describes Hagar's weeping, but then reports that it is Ishmael's cry that God hears. Is this a conflation of mother and son? Or is the text reflecting a preferential treatment toward the son (i.e., the male figure)? One can reconcile the two questions by suggesting that God is responding to Hagar's request in saving her child. God did not ignore Hagar, but directed the response to the cries of the mother's son. Once again we see that the mother puts her son before herself and her needs.

The meaning of Hagar's name may be significant. There are two main interpretations of the root. One points to the ancient Arabic origins of the name, while the other connects the name with the Arabic *hajara*, meaning variously, "to flee" and "fugitive."[24] Whatever the root connection, Hagar's name refers to her future banishment, as well as speaks to the identity of her descendents. Her son becomes, according to biblical tradition, the forefather of the Arab peoples (Gen.16:11–12; 21:18–21), and she the matriarch of a nation. Ishmael's name also deserves comment. She is told to name her son "Ishmael . . . for the LORD has paid heed to [her] suffering . . ." (16:11). Ishmael's name means, "God hears," and the name refers to Hagar and Ishmael's experience in the wilderness.

Hagar represents different images to many people. The text presents Hagar as the 'woman scorned,' and rejected women seem to identify with her. As Trible states, "she is the faithful maid exploited, the black woman used by the male and abused by the female of the ruling class, the surrogate mother, the resident alien, the runaway youth . . . and the pregnant young woman alone."[25] Yet, is Hagar only a symbol of marginalization as many scholars paint her? Some scholars point out that Hagar's fate in the end is quite favorable. She is the only character to venture to name the deity (Gen. 16:13). And she bears a son who becomes the leader of a clan, then nation. These experiences alone qualify her to be a character of central importance.

Hagar is a distinct figure in Genesis in that her motherhood comes about not by her own choice, but rather is the result of a decision on the part of her mistress. Her case highlights a phenomenon discussed by Miriam Johnson, who discusses women who emerge as weak wives versus those who operate as strong mothers.[26] The Hagar story is a case of a woman on a low rung of the societal ladder who nearly usurps the authority of her privileged mistress by producing offspring. Though Hagar never becomes the dominant wife, nor her son the leading heir, she nevertheless, emerges as a sympathetic character and her son comes into a sizable inheritance. Hagar's account provides an interesting addition to our discussion on Genesis mothers.

REBECCA

The next female figuration of a mother we encounter is Rebecca (Rivkah). She first appears a pure, unselfish, loving young teenager, and becomes a decisive mature woman with great strength of mind.[27] Rebecca develops into the most active and powerful of the four mothers. Do we wonder if her name has any bearing on her life experience? If we accept that metathesis (the interchange of letters) has occurred in the root of Rebecca's name, then the meaning of her name connects her to the other matriarchs (excepting Sarah, whose name is connected with "ruling" and "prevailing"). The root letters of Rivkah, *r-b-q*, mean, "to stall," or "to tie with rope." If metathesis has taken place then the name could be connected with *baqar*, meaning "cattle."[28] Other mothers of Genesis also have names relating to husbandry, which speaks to the social setting of the semi-nomadic tribes of ancient Israel. Although we in the modern age have lost sight of the significance and even attractiveness of herds and flocks of cattle and sheep, the ancients evidently often relied heavily on animal imagery to describe objects of great beauty and value.²⁹ Therefore it should come as no surprise that the mothers of Bible are often named for flora and fauna. The great importance attached to husbandry as a financial necessity and social way of life is reflected in the matriarch's names. Perhaps this economic and social importance attributed to the animals they are named for is mirrored in the influence these mothers had on the ancient Israelite community.

At this juncture in the patriarchal narratives, Abraham, now old, must secure an heir to inherit the land. Abraham does not want his son Isaac to intermarry with the people of the land, the Canaanites, nor does he want Isaac to leave the land himself. He feels the appropriate time has come to arrange a marriage. Abraham calls his steward and instructs him to go back to Nahor, Abraham's former dwelling place, to find a wife for Isaac among his kinsmen.³⁰ Abraham's two primary concerns, love of land and concern for continuity, would both be fulfilled by a prospective marriage. The fruit of the marriage would provide progeny to inherit the land.

The choice of the future mother of Abraham's grandchildren is therefore a carefully undertaken project, with a qualifying test of her personality. Abraham's steward encounters Rebecca by the well at the outskirts of town. He is impressed by her hospitable welcome. She offers water to him and to all of his thirsty animals, and, in addition, generously invites him to her parents' home for food and rest. As an aside, Rivka, whose name conjures up "cattle" and the idea of a "stall," here acts not as the shepherded, but rather as the shepherd by caring for animals in need. Unknowingly to her, she has passed all of Eliezer's tests. The emissary explains his matchmaking mission to the family who come to believe the marriage was decreed in heaven. Rebecca's mother and brother together request a fortnight preparation before Rebecca's departure but Rebecca, when notified of the proposal, insists on leaving immediately (Gen. 24:58). Rebecca's willingness to set out for an unknown destination displays her daring and foreshadows the risks she will later take as wife and mother. That she even early on appears to be a woman of strength of will indicates the kind of mother she will later become.

The uniqueness of the Rebecca betrothal scene is that the groom, Isaac, is absent. Compare this scene with later betrothal scenes at a well. Jacob and Moses are not only present in their meeting scenes but also demonstrate their initiative. Jacob draws water for all of the shepherds who are not able to "roll the stone from the well's mouth" (Gen. 29:1–12). Moses defends the daughters of Jethro against the shepherds and also waters their flock (Ex. 2:17). In the Rebecca story, however, she is the one to draw the water and to refresh the guest. She is the one to jump on the opportunity to marry. Her initial assertiveness prepares us for her active role as wife and mother. Indeed, the decisive verb "to go" (Heb. *h-l-kh*) occurs seven times in connection with Rebecca,[31] which seems to suggest she was actively engaged in life, always looking to move forward.

Isaac's acceptance of Rebecca as his wife bridges the lingering influence of the first matriarch, Sarah, with the exploding power of the second. "He brought Rebecca into his mother Sarah's tent, and took Rebecca, and she became his wife and he loved her; and Isaac was comforted after his mother's death" (Gen. 24:67). The rabbis further the connection, "You find that as long as Sarah lived, a cloud [of God] hung over her tent; when she died, that cloud disappeared; but when Rebecca came, it returned." A midrash claims that Rebecca continued all the religious rituals that Sarah had practiced.[32] Thus, tradition holds that Rebecca was as righteous as Sarah had been.

Rebecca's life as wife and mother is characterized by continual turbulence. She faces the same problem of barrenness as many other biblical women. After Isaac prays to God for his wife to conceive, God grants his request, but Rebecca's pregnancy is difficult. We read, "The children struggled together within her causing her to cry out, 'If it be so, why do I exist?' and she went to inquire of God" (Gen. 25:22). The oracle informs her of the divergent destinies of the twin sons she is carrying. "Two nations are in your womb and two separate people shall issue from you. One people shall be stronger than the other people and the older shall serve the younger." When the sons grow up "Esau became a skillful hunter, a man of the outdoors; but Jacob was a mild man who stayed in camp. Isaac loved Esau while Rebecca loved Jacob" (Gen. 26:22–28). The warring within the womb foreshadowed the brothers' future conflict. The activities within her womb also influence later decisions she makes.

Two pivotal scenes displaying decisive encounters between the two brothers reveal Rebecca's complex relationship to her sons. The earlier scene describes an interaction between Jacob and Esau. Esau returning home ravenously hungry from hunting sells his birthright to Jacob in exchange for supper. The second scene describes Isaac beckoning Esau to his side, requesting him to hunt and prepare game so Isaac can eat and bless Esau before Isaac dies. Rebecca learns of Isaac's intentions and, willing to foil her husband, devises a plan to obtain the blessing for her beloved Jacob. We can only speculate whether she knew anything about the lentil soup-for-birthright exchange that had taken place earlier. In any case, while she did not have the legal authority to give Jacob the blessing herself, she did have power within the domestic realm to manipulate events to fulfill her own understanding of God's plan for Jacob's destiny as bearer of the covenant. This episode underscores the authority possessed by the father to bless, but also points to the unofficial power discussed above held by the mother, to orchestrate events which affected the entire household, and ultimately the destiny of the Jewish people.

Women may not have hierarchical status, but they were able to wield great influence behind the scenes in their own way.

Even at an early juncture in the Rebecca and Isaac narrative, Rebecca displays the leadership, energy, and strength that her husband Isaac lacks. She is the forceful personality in her sons development and growth. She has more ambition than Isaac with regard to their future success. She is the dominant planner and the proactive figure in the narrative. Is Rebecca compensating for weakness on Isaac's part? Certainly Isaac is not presented within biblical tradition as a dynamic personality, but rather, a sideline observer who watches the action taking place. Early on his mother, Sarah, takes charge in molding his future, by casting out his half-brother and possible competition for birthright (Gen.21:9–13). He then is led by his father to be sacrificed, apparently never protesting his father's obedience to this seemingly incomprehensible command. Finally, later, it is Isaac's wife, Rebecca, who influences which of his sons received his blessing. Isaac emerges in the tradition as a figure constantly under the influence of his family members, and provides us an interesting foil to the more powerful personality of his wife Rebecca.

With her characteristic vision and determination, Rebecca orders Jacob to choose two good kids before Esau could return from the hunt. She conspires to prepare them herself as the tasty meal Isaac requested. Jacob protests that his father would easily detect the physical difference between his smooth skin and his brother's hairy arms, and would thereby curse rather than bless him. Rebecca allays his fears with the encouraging words "Let your curse be upon me, my son. Only obey my voice and go fetch me them" (Gen. 27:13). Their deception of Isaac succeeds. By the time Esau arrives for the blessing, he finds that Jacob has preceded him and cries bitterly. Esau vows that when his father dies, he will kill Jacob. Rebecca construes a plan to send Jacob away to find a wife, explaining to Isaac that she does not want Jacob to follow in Esau's footsteps and to intermarry with the daughters of the land (Gen. 27:46). Jacob is thus able to depart immediately after receiving his father's blessing and to escape his brother's wrath.

The temptation of the modern reader of the Rebecca narrative is to judge her for loving one son more the other. However, does a close reading of the text show that she cared for both her sons? Nuanced within the text is evidence suggesting that she loved both Jacob and Esau. Genesis 28:5 records Rebecca as the "mother of Jacob and Esau." The deliberate mention of Esau along with Jacob in a passage describing the future plans of Jacob suggests that Rebecca cared for both her children. So why does she favor Jacob? Perhaps the overwhelming influence on Rebecca is the oracle she receives from God during her pregnancy (26:22–24). At that time she learns that her sons might war against one another and that the older would be ruled by the younger. Though she clearly loves both her sons, she feels responsible to help secure the birthright for the younger son, because of the divine oracle communicated to her long ago. She may even have feared harm to her son Esau were he to have retained the birthright, since that would have gone against God's wishes. Her plan to send Jacob away not only prevents Jacob's murder; it also prevents Esau from becoming a murderer. That tragedy would have led to her being bereaved of both of them in one day (Gen. 28:45).[33] Thus, one reading of the text seems to support the notion that Rebecca behaved in a manipulative way that would bring about the best for both her sons. Within the patriarchal system in which she lived, Rebecca operated within the ambit of her household to bring about favorable ends to all those she loved.

When Rebecca sends her son Jacob to the home of her brother, Laban, we see her as self-sacrificing, willing to part from her favorite son to promote his career as the successor to the divine promise made to Abraham and Isaac. She hopes Jacob will return when his brother's anger abates. And she hopes Esau proves himself successful in other areas. We may also suspect that she knows her brother, Laban's, exploitative character. Perhaps she knows that Jacob will pay his dues under his uncle's tutelage, and in this way, serve a period of atonement for his undeniable part in a subterfuge. For her part, she will suffer the pain of his absence. We may further speculate that in the years of Jacob's absence, Rebecca is able to explain to Esau what happened and why. The generous manner in which Esau and Jacob meet years later, suggests Esau's change of heart. "Esau ran to meet him, took him in his arms and fell on his neck and kissed him, and they both wept" (Gen. 33:5). We may assume that the entire family became reconciled with one another to some extent. We are told that Isaac was 180 years old when he died and that both his sons buried him (Gen. 35:27–29). Unfortunately, the text never mentions whether Rebecca is ever reunited with either of her sons. We might believe that the price Rebecca pays for her part in any ploy is to never see her sons again.[34] But perhaps a more optimistic view is that Rebecca, so instrumental in her sons' destinies, also plays a large part in their future reconciliation. The text is silent, but what is recorded invites one to speculate on Rebecca's role in the reunification.

In evaluating the story of Rebecca's relationship to her sons, let us review significant encounters depicted in the text of Chapter 27:6–14 where this mother's plan is outlined. Why is she more aware of her sons' characteristics and qualities than her husband? The explanation may lie in that a mother represents the realm of the home, the place of care and nurturing. We are told that Isaac was "old and his eyes were so weak, he could not see." He was not only physically blind but perhaps spiritually unaware of the strengths and weaknesses of his sons (Gen. 27–1). Therefore, because of Isaac's impairments, perhaps only Rebecca could be the instrument of God to carry out the divine convenantal plans. God uses her to transfer blessings and transmit the tradition to future generations. She certainly is utilized by God on behalf of her sons in a way Isaac never was.

Rebecca's deception as a mother poses a moral problem for some, and it is even more difficult to understand that her son and the future bearer of our tradition, Jacob, would not have the integrity to protest his mother's ruse. The prophets Hosea and Jeremiah allude disapprovingly to Jacob's treatment of Esau (Hos. 12:3–4; Jer. 9:3). While modern critics find fault with Rebecca for her actions,[35] since it is she who initiates the act of deception, the biblical text itself does not condemn her (Gen. 27:5–6). On the contrary, it claims that her actions are in harmony with God's plan as put forth in the oracle. The detailed descriptions of the deceit revolve around Rebecca while Jacob plays the role of the obedient son. My contention is that Rebecca deceives Isaac not because she is a devious wife, but because she has less authority in the household, and this was the only way she could implement God's plan, as she understood it. Though her behavior may not be an entirely positive role model, she emerges as a matriarch who earned the trust of her son, Jacob, to the extent that he puts his life and integrity on the line. At the same time, we cannot exclude the possibility that Rebecca was likewise concerned with Esau's destiny though this relationship is not emphasized in the text. We speculate that her positive influence is best attested in the eventual reconciliation of the two brothers. Hence, Rebecca acted not out of deceit, but out of desperation, using cunning and insight within the hierarchical structure in which she lived to achieve God's plan put forth in the oracle. As we pointed out previously, Rebecca does not hold legal authority to issue the first-born blessing, yet she uses what power she could to maneuver the system. She faithfully works to implement the prophecy that she received when she was pregnant.

The narrative portrays this mother developing from a young women, to becoming a budding mother, and finally emerging as a formidable matriarch. Surprisingly, she unfolds as the strongest figure in this narrative, towering over four men: first Eliezar, then Isaac, then her two sons, Jacob and Esau. The story of Rebecca demonstrates that the biblical mother could be a forceful personality, even within a limited and androcentric arena.

RACHEL AND LEAH

Rachel and Leah are introduced together as Laban's daughters. Later we see jealousy emerge between the two siblings and we speculate that this jealousy may have come about because of their differing physical appearances and individual struggles with motherhood. Even as young girls, we already hear of their differences: "Laban had two daughters: the name of the elder was Leah, and the name of the younger was Rachel. Leah had weak eyes; but Rachel was beautiful and well favored" (Gen. 29:16). Most biblical translations render the Hebrew word describing Leah's eyes as *rakot*, "weak," as if she had poor vision, or her eyes lacked luster. According to the Talmud, beautiful, clear eyes were a woman's most distinguishing mark of beauty.[36] More recent translations inform that *rakh* could also mean tender and soft, rather than weak,[37] suggesting that Leah had a sensitive personality with internal charm and cow-like eyes. Leah's sister, Rachel, is unambiguously described as both shapely and beautiful (Gen. 29:16–17).[38] The two Hebrew expressions used to describe her appearance are synonyms and this double description might indicate not only her physical beauty but her spiritual beauty as well.

Jacob finds himself in the home of Rachel and Leah, after his mother had sent him away to escape the wrath of his elder brother (Gen. 27). Unlike Abraham in the previous generation who had sent his steward to contract a marriage for his son Isaac, here it is Rebecca, the mother, who orchestrates the matchmaking. That Rebecca is involved in the marriage arrangement of her son, usually a function of the patriarch of the family, again shows that the mother had unassigned power. She wishes for him to acquire a wife from the ancestral family to fulfill the promise of the covenant. Again, it is at a well where Jacob meets Rachel, and so begins a love story unparalleled in the biblical narrative (Gen. 29:1–12). Jacob is a poor stranger, his own emissary, a refugee from his brother's wrath. He bears no rich gifts as his father's steward had brought, and walks alone, with no flock to proclaim his wealth. As a prospective suitor all he can offer are his qualities and abilities. He advertises his worth by flaunting his physical strength and rolls the heavy stone that covers the mouth of the well by himself so that the flocks could drink[39] (Gen. 29: 9–11).

Jacob introduces himself, boldly kisses Rachel, and tells her that he is a kinsman. Except for in the "Song of Songs," Jacob's kiss is the only explicit biblical scene of a man kissing a woman. Jacob asks Laban for Rachel as his wife, and because of his deep love for her, agrees to the condition that he work for her father for seven years. The text adds, "Jacob worked for Rachel seven years and they seemed in his eyes as a few days because of the great love he felt for her" (Gen. 29:20). Such a description of love is exceptional in the Bible. Jacob's sensitive streak seen here may well have come from his mother's influence. His ease at expressing emotion suggests an understanding that one receives from contact with a strong and loving woman.

Ironically, the great love Jacob has for Rachel does not quench her thirst for motherhood. She still yearns to give birth, which underscores the importance and prestige granted the mother in ancient Israel. Clearly, Jacob preferred Rachel. Though he is deceived on his wedding night, Jacob loved Rachel until the end of her life. He even recalls her on his deathbed (Gen.48:7). There is an unusual dynamic in this love triangle between Jacob, Leah and Rachel. Ironically, though progeny has top priority in the lives of the matriarchs, the fecund wife is the less-favored one, while the barren wife is the more beloved. With the cultural emphasis on the value of bearing children, one would expect the reverse.[40] Perhaps this account shows that men in ancient Israel were unaffected and uninfluenced by the mother-dynamic that was so powerful in female circles. Men were more concerned with perseverance of the family line, while women sought to have greater power in the domestic realm through their sons.

The jealousy and rivalry between the two sisters over bearing children echoes the earlier antagonism we previously discussed regarding Sarah and Hagar. "When Rachel saw that she had borne Jacob no children, she became envious of her sister" (Gen: 30:1). Leah and Rachel are in a continuous competition to become mothers, and thus gain recognition in a patrilineal society. At this stage of the narrative, each woman feels unappreciated: Leah for not being loved and Rachel for not having born children.

Leah has four sons, the name of each indicate her desire to be loved by her husband.[41] When Leah bore her first son she names him Reuben for she declares, "God has seen my suffering [and gave me a son], and now my husband will love me" (Gen. 29: 32). Although the names of her first four sons express Leah's desperate longing for love, only Reuben proactively pursues to bring about this end. Leah's naming of Reuben reflects her experience vis-à-vis her husband and her desire that the birth of a son would change the marital dynamics. Does Reuben's name describe the nature of his relationship with his mother? Her initial proclamation of joy seems to foreshadow a loving relationship that would later ensue. However, Leah, even in her hopeful optimism in naming her sons, never acquires the love she sought from her husband. Reuben repeatedly tries to elevate the status of his mother, as we will show.

In the interim, Rachel, still barren and observing her sister's fecundity, becomes extremely jealous. Rachel's envy erupts in a confrontation with her husband. Rachel cries out "Give me children or I shall die" (Gen. 30:1–3). Jacob responds, "Am I God that I can give you children?" Many find it hard to understand how Jacob could react so callously to the pain of his beloved wife. Rachel's request is justifiable, remembering the concern shown by Isaac when he prayed for his barren wife Rebecca. Likewise, Abraham was compassionate about Sarah's suffering over her barrenness when he accepted her offer of the handmaid to produce a son. Perhaps Jacob's reaction indicates that he feels quite helpless, and her attack makes him feel more so. Still, why could Jacob not have responded by saying "I will pray for you to God, as my father did for my mother?" But not only does Jacob fail to show sympathy for her plight, he rebukes her and disclaims any responsibility for her tragic condition. Perhaps because Jacob is already a father of many sons, he does not understand the tragic predicament of her sterility. This account seems to underscore the intrinsic difference in role and responsibility between men and women of the Bible. While married or single men could acquire honor through meritorious behavior, women are portrayed as seeing marriage and motherhood as their one trump card; only by bearing children would they achieve status and recognition and acquire a measure of power. The pain and desperation of Rachel's request must be viewed in the context of biblical times when the key to the woman's power came through producing progeny.

The unique episode of the mandrakes further illustrates Rachel's desperate attempts to become a mother (Genesis 35:22). One day at the time of the wheat harvest, Reuben, Leah's eldest son, came upon mandrakes in the field and, in keeping with his concern over his mother's despondence over her lesser status, brought her the mandrakes in order to comfort her. Why would a son bring a plant believed to possess aphrodisiac properties to his mother? Is he expressing sympathy for his mother, who is an unloved wife? As we speculated, Reuben is painfully aware of his mother's affliction as the less-preferred wife. Mandrakes are fleshy plants, referred to as "love apples," believed both to contain aphrodisiac properties, and also thought to be a cure for barrenness. Rachel asks Leah, "Please give me some of your son's mandrakes" (Gen. 30:14). Leah responds "Is it not enough for you to take away my husband, that you should take away my son's mandrakes?" Rachel bribes her sister to give her the mandrakes, and so to help her conceive, and in exchange, allows Leah to spend the night with Jacob. The deal was done, and the result of Leah's encounter with Jacob is another two sons, Issachar and Zebulun (Gen. 30:18–22). Noteworthy in this account is Jacob's apparent willingness to play the pawn in his wives' fight for fertility. His tolerance of their bickering must once again be understood in its proper context. The underlying social pressure placed upon women to bear children was immense and offered women their one avenue of power. Women as mothers take center stage in the stories of the birthing of the tribes of ancient Israel.

While Leah is plagued by insecurity of her husband's affection, Rachel is secure in her knowledge of her husband's love for her, but suffers from the lack of bearing children. God eventually does "remember Rachel" who will bear a son, Joseph, meaning, "the Lord shall add to me another son" (Gen. 30:22). As is often the case, the chosen name for Joseph reflects not his character, but speaks to Rachel's desire for future children. Indeed, she will bear one more son, whom she names Benoni, "the son of my suffering," but sadly, she dies while giving birth to him (Gen. 35:19). Again, the name Benoni addresses the experience of the parents not the child. Rachel expresses her lifelong struggle with barrenness in her naming speech, while Jacob, renaming his son Benjamin, expresses his hope that the newborn will go on to achieve a place of position. Rachel's great desire for children is telling. Though she has the devotion of her husband, she still remains unsatisfied. She realizes that only through her progeny would she be able to wield real influence within the domestic realm. As long as she remains childless, she lacks personal contentment and power within the household.

Rachel's death had a great impact on Jacob's household, sparking struggles between father and son over the status of the remaining mothers. According to Genesis 35:22, Reuben has sexual relations with his father's concubine Bilhah after Rachel's death. His father seems very vexed by his action, and later removes him from having the privileges of the firstborn (Gen. 49:3ff; Deut.33:6; 1 Chron.5:1). The rebellious behavior of the son has been interpreted by some contemporary scholars as Reuben's attempt to become head of the household, not merely defending his mother's honor.[42] This act of aggression may show how strongly Reuben felt for his mother. Reuben is punished in the biblical text, and later tradition also views his actions unfavorably, but tries to downplay the gravity of his sin.

The Talmud takes the view that Reuben's behavior was not physical, but symbolic: "If my mother's sister was a rival to my mother, must the maid of my mother's sister be a rival to my mother" (b. Sabb 55b)? Reuben, Leah's loyal eldest son, attempted once again, as in the previous mandrake episode, to force Jacob to return to Leah's tent and atone for years of what his mother felt to be humiliating rejection, and to restore some justice to his mother's life. Rashi, the leading rabbinic exegete of the 11th century, follows the traditional rabbinic explanation in his comments on this verse. Reuben's behavior offended the medieval commentator who translates the word *vayishkav* not as "sleeping with" Bilhah, but rather as "placing the bed" of his mother Leah in Rachel's tent where Jacob always slept.[43] Thus medieval scholars explain that Reuben's violation of Bilhah, Rachel's handmaid, was to avenge his mother's honor. Accordingly, Reuben wished to ascertain that Bilhah would not supplant or even rival his own mother's position as chief wife now that Rachel was dead.

Reuben's futile and rash efforts to secure status for his mother Leah bore little fruit as Jacob's deep love for Rachel was transferred to Rachel's son Joseph and the youngest son, whom Jacob renames Benjamin, "son of my right hand." In fact, Reuben hurt his position and lost his right of the first born for his antagonism towards his father.[44] But do we know anything about Rachel's relationship with her son, Joseph? Unfortunately we have no information on this matter from the narrative. According to the story, she never lived to see or raise her youngest son, Benjamin.

Perhaps Rachel's mothering qualities are recognized by the late biblical prophet Jeremiah. In later biblical tradition, ironically Rachel, who experienced great struggle with fertility, assumes a larger role than any individual mother, becoming the Mother of all Israel who weeps for her children when they go into exile.[45] Jeremiah's prophecy allows Rachel to transcend time. Her voice rises from the dead to cry on behalf of her exiled children.

> "A voice was heard in Ramah, lamentation, and bitter weeping; Rachel weeping for her children refused to be comforted for her children, because they were not. Thus said the LORD: Refrain your voice from weeping and your eyes from tears; for your work shall be rewarded. . . . There is hope in your end, says the LORD, that your children shall come again to their own border."(Jer.31:14–17).

Throughout the centuries Rachel would also become the symbol of hope for barren women who made the pilgrimage to her tomb and prayed to conceive.[46]

Perhaps in closing this section on Leah and Rachel we can mention the handmaids, Zilpah and Bilhah, who are also mothers, at least biologically. They birthed tribes and their sons had equal share in the inheritance with the sons of Leah and Rachel. Zilpah bore Gad and Asher, while Bilhah bore Dan and Naphtali. Sadly, the text does not record any interaction they had with their children. What seems clear is that only recognized mothers (i.e., Leah and Rachel) received unassigned power within the domestic realm. Zilpah and Bilhah, who loaned their wombs to their respective mistresses, remain throughout their lives as handmaids without real power.

SUMMARY OF THE FIRST MOTHERS OF GENESIS

We started our chapter focusing on Eve as the proverbial "mother of all living," and positive archetype of motherhood. We choose not to focus on the pain of birth, but rather opted to highlight the subsequent joy experienced when Eve "acquired a male" with God's help. Her later experiences with motherhood were marred by tragedy, when one son dies and the other is cursed. Perhaps Eve's experiences with motherhood led the matriarchs of Genesis to promote the welfare of their children and protect the rights of their sons. Sarah devotes all her energy to ensure that Isaac will retain legal rights as Abraham's heir. Rebecca's strategic advice to Jacob about obtaining his father's blessing evokes many responses, both positive and negative, in regard to the morality of her behavior. In any case, Jacob's compliance suggests that his mother had earned Jacob's trust; he was willing to place his destiny in her hands. In Jeremiah's prophecies, the figure of Rachel comes to symbolize the praying mother who cares for all the Children of Israel.[47] Because she strives during her lifetime to bear children, claiming that she would rather die than be childless, it is tragic that she does indeed die in Ephrath giving birth to her second son. As a kind of tribute, ancient Jewish legend tells that Jacob intentionally buries Rachel in Ephrath, having foreseen that his descendents would pass by on their way to exile and that she would weep and pray for them (Jer. 31:14–6).[48] It is thus fitting that her name represents the mother's praying for the return of an exiled nation. While Leah appears more concerned with obtaining the love of her husband than with bearing children, she too is depicted as gaining her children's loyalty, especially that of Reuben, who as the eldest speaks for all the others. The actions of Reuben may be indicative of how sons defended their mother in a patriarchal society, and explains why women longed for sons. There is a reoccurring paradigm in the text of strong mothers who defend their sons who, in turn, express their devotion and loyalty. Even more, the sons carry out the wishes of their mother in the public, official realm, and act as an extension of the mothers' voice and vision. In the androcentric world in which they lived, the mothers of Genesis found power through their sons.

All these women are forever tied to each other in the tradition as the founding mothers of a future nation. They possess similar strengths and undergo parallel struggles, yet emerge as unique individuals. Each mother discussed above values her son's interests more than anything else. They are all single-minded in purpose: they want to see their sons achieve great success at almost any cost. Is it appropriate, and even preferable, then to view these women as set in a distinct framework, to think of these women as "mothers of great men"? Though they certainly are profoundly connected to one another by shared purpose and destiny, they are best examined and appreciated as individuals who encountered unique experiences. To bracket them together seems to do an injustice to their uniqueness. Above we have gone to great lengths to show that each woman should be studied on her own merit. While we may reference her forerunners to better understand her actions and make comparisons, in the end, Eve, Adah, Zillah, Sarah, Hagar, Rebecca, Leah and Rachel deserve singular recognition for their admirable characteristics and actions.

NOTES

1. Phyllis Trible, *God and the Rhetoric of Sexuality*, (Philadelphia: Fortress Press, 1978), 94–121ff. "Depatriarchalizing in Biblical Tradition" in *The Jewish Woman*, ed.

by Elizabeth Koltun (New York: Schoken Books, 1978), pp. 217–240. Ilana Pardes, *Countertraditions in the Bible: A Feminist Approach* (Cambridge, Massachusetts: Harvard University Press, 1992), 13–37. Athalya Brenner, *The Israelite Woman* (Sheffield: JSOT Press, 1985); J.Cheryl Exum, *Fragented Women* (Valley Forge, PA: Trinity Press International, 1993); See also Leila Leah Bronner, *From Eve to Esther* (Louisville, Kentucky: Westminster John Knox Press, 1994), 22–41.

2. Martin Rose, "Names of God in the OT" (*Anchor Bible Dictionary*: Vol. 4, New York: Doubleday, 1992), 1002

3. Mieke Bal, *Lethal Love: Feminist Literary Interpretations of Biblical Love Stories* (Bloomington: Indiana University Press, 1987), 128.

4. See E.A. Speiser, *Genesis*, (Garden City, New York: Doubleday and Company, Inc., 1964), 29, for a different translation: "And she [Eve] conceived and bore Cain saying, 'I have added a life with the help of Yahweh.' " This verse is variously interpreted in many different translations of the Bible. See Nahum Sarna, *JPS Torah Commentary* (New York: Jewish Publication Society, 1989), 32.

5. Adrienne Rich, *Of Women Born* (New York: Norton & Co., 1986), 159.

6. Ilana Pardes, *Counterraditions in the Bible: A Feminist Approach* (Cambridge: Harvard University Press, 1992), 47–48

7. Scholars speculate that Eve's naming speech might have mythological overtones from Near Eastern goddess stories of creation. See Ilana Pardes, *Op. Cit.*, p. 45.

8. According to Ilana Pardes, the namegiver is male in about seventeen cases, whereas there are twenty-seven cases of female namegivers. See Ilana Pardes, *Op. Cit.*, p. 163.

9. Since my interest is in the final form of the text, I do not distinguish documentary sources here and elsewhere but for those interested in these problems of authorship see Speiser, op. cited, XXXVII–XXXXIII.

10. This song of Lamech has also been interpreted as Lamech boasting to his wives that he took a man's life, though that person only inflicted a bruise on him. Thus interpreted, the song is a song boasting of murder and the growth of the spirit of Cain.

11. *Genesis Rab.* xxiii: 4–5.

12. See Speiser, *Genesis*, op. cited, 119–21, for further discussion of the custom of surrogate motherhood.

13. We will continue our discussion of Hagar below; here the concern is with Sarah.

14. Ur-Nammu (2112–2095 B.C.E.) mentions the case of a slave woman who, "comparing herself to her mistress, speaks insolently to her" or strikes her, and Hammurabi's laws deals with the situation of the female slave-concubine who "has claimed equality with her mistress because she bore children." See note on Genesis 16:2 (p. 117) in the *JPS Torah Commentary: Genesis* by Nahum Sarna.

15. Isaac's name, from the root *z-h-k*, means "laughter," and is related to *mezachek*, the word under discussion. Isaac was so-named because of Sarah's initial reaction when she heard she would give birth in her old age.

16. Genesis Rab. 53.11; Tosef.Sot.6:6; RH 18b.

17. Savina Teubal, "Sarah and Hagar: Matriarchs and Visionaries" (in *A Feminist Companion to Genesis* edited by Athaya Brenner. Sheffield: Sheffield Academic Press, 1993), 235–250.

18. *Yalkut Shimoni*, Vol. 1 (Midrashic commentary to the Bible), (Jerusalem, Israel: Monson, 1962), para.98.

19. *Pirke de,R. Eliezar*, (Pseudepigraphic Midrash on Bible) (Jerusalem, Israel: Jacob Bamberg), Chap. 72, 13.

20. Phillis Trible has a discussion about Sarah's involvement in the Akedah. See "Genesis 22: the Sacrifice of Sarah" (In *Not in Heaven: Coherence and Complexity in Biblical Narrative*, ed. Jason P. Rosenblatt and Joseph C. Sitterson, Bloomington: Indiana University Press, 1992), 170–191.

21. *Midrash Rabbah*, (London: Soncino Press, 1983), Vol.II, 538

22. We are using the names Sarah and Abraham throughout, although in these verses God renamed both of them, from Avram to Abraham, and from Sarai to Sarah (Genesis 17:4 and 17:15).

23. Though Hagar is often seen as the "concubine" of Abraham, significantly the text uses the word, "wife" to describe her relationship with him (See Genesis. 16:3).

24. For more on the Arabic connections of the name, see the article, "Hagar," by E. Knauf in the *Anchor Bible Dictionary*, Vol.3 (New York: Doubleday, 1992),18–19; For the connection of Hagar with *hajara*, see N.Sarna, *The JPS Torah Commentary: Genesis* (New York: JPS Press, 1989), 119

25. Phyllis Trible, *Texts of Terror* (Philadelphia: Fortress Press, 1984), 28.

26. Miriam M. Johnson, *Strong Mothers, Weak Wives* (Berkeley: University of California Press, 1988), 6.

27. See Genesis 24 for the courtship of Isaac and Rebecca.

28. A.Beck, "Rebekah," in the *Anchor Bible Dictionary*, Vol.5 (New York: Doubleday, 1992), 629

29. Beck, 629.

30. Elsewhere the steward is named Eliezer of Damascus (Genesis 15).

31. N.Sarna, *Genesis*, 161

32. *Genesis Rab.* 60:16.

33. Compare II Samuel 14:4–17.

34. Genesis 49:31 mentions that Rebecca was buried with her husband as well as with the other patriarchs in the cave of Machpelah.

35. Susan Niditch, *Underdogs and Tricksters: A Prelude to Biblical Folklore* (San Francisco: Harper and Row, 1987) 96; Carol Newsom and Sharon Ringe, eds.*The Women's Bible Commentary* (London: Westminster/John Knox Press, 1992), 15.

36. The Talmud states: "So long as her eyes are beautiful her body needs no examination." (*b.Ta'anit* 24a).

37. E.A. Speiser, *Genesis*, op. cited, 225.

38. As mentioned earlier, their names mean cow and ewe respectively. Some scholars want to see in the names cow and ewe an indication of later generations' jockeying for position between cattle herders and sheep herders in the early tribes of Israel; see *Harper's Bible Dictionary* (San Francisco, California: Harper & Row, Publishers, 1971), 552.

39. Compare Exodus 2:17.

40. This same dynamic is found in the story between Elkanah, his beloved but barren wife Hannah, and his second wife Penina, Samuel 1:1–6.

41. Reuven's name is discussed in the text. For the meanings of the names "Simeon," "Levi," and "Judah," see Genesis 29:31–5.

42. *Anchor Dictionary*, Vol. 5 (New York, New York: Doubleday & Co., 1992), 693, s.v. Reuben.

43. Rashi to Genesis 35:22.

44. See Genesis 49:4 where Jacob rebukes Reuben for his rash behavior claiming that his temper led him to defy his father's honor. See Genesis 35:22 as discussed above.

45. Rachel's role here in Jeremiah 31:15ff reminds us of the National Mother, whose role and identity we address in a later chapter.

46. See Susan Starr Sered, "A Tale of Three Rachels, or The Cultural Herstory of A Symbol," *Nashim: A Journal of Jewish Women's Studies and Gender Issues*, no. 1 (Jerusalem, Israel: The Schechter Institute of Jewish Studies, 1998), 8, 16, 36–37, which demonstrates the mechanisms of myth making around women, especially the Biblical Rachel who became a metaphor for God's promise to return the nation from exile in Babylon to the land of Zion.

47. Both Rachel and Leah are mentioned as the matriarchs of Israel in Ruth 4:11.

48. Rabbi David Kimchi (RaDaK) on Jeremiah 31:16 in *Mikraot Gedolot*, 139.

Chapter Two

Mothers of a Budding Nation

He places the childless woman in her household as a happy mother of children.

Psalm 113:9

A noble mother must have bred so brave a son.

CAMPBELL, *Napoleon and the British Sailor*

In the last chapter, we focused on the first mothers, primarily concentrating on the three barren matriarchs mentioned in Genesis who after much struggle successfully conceive. Now we analyze three other barren women whose journeys toward motherhood are featured in the early historical books of Judges, Samuel, and Kings.[1] These sources offer some impressive images of mothers: Samson's mother (Judges 13–16), Samuel's mother Hannah (I Sam. 1–2), and the Shunammite woman (II Kings 4:9–38), and the lesser-known mother of Jabez (1 Chron.4:9). The mothers above all contribute to the development of their sons, men who were destined to play a leading role in the life of a newly formed nation. To a lesser degree, we also look at four mothers who appear briefly but who seem to have a negative influence on their sons. We analyze these negative female figures in order to show that both admirable and unsavory characters contributed to the growth of the budding nation. By including all the above-mentioned mothers in our study, we hope to offer a comprehensive picture of mothers in ancient Israel.

Before moving on, as an aside we should make a comment about barrenness within the Bible. Why do so many women struggle with conceiving a child? As we saw in the last chapter, the matriarchs wrestled with the problem of childlessness, finally overcoming their predicaments by giving birth to men who go on to become great leaders. In this chapter we encounter the barren woman motif, but perhaps with a different angle than seen in the last chapter. We can view the barren motif in a few ways. First the question of who controlled the forces of fertility was an important one in the ancient world. The stories of the barren woman functioned to show that the gift of life comes from God alone.[2] The barren stories may also perform as a literary device used to show the obstacles encountered in the birth of a "hero." The text builds drama by showing how each obstacle could be overcome and the promise of progeny eventually fulfilled.[3] Lastly, biblical characters, both male and female, experience growth through hardship and distress. Women who are initially childless often undergo character development in their quest to conceive.

SAMSON'S MOTHER

The dramatic story of Samson recounts an instance of a child being dedicated by his mother to the service of God. While most studies focus on his amorous relations with women, the focus is here on Samson's relationship to his mother. The biblical narrative contrasts the righteous Israelite mother with three foreign women. The circumstances of his birth augur an unusual destiny. Scripture describes an angel appearing before the wife of a man named Manoah telling her that she will bear a child. He instructs her not to drink any wine or other intoxicant, nor to eat unclean food, and stipulates that the child must also not drink wine nor any strong drink nor eat any unclean thing; no razor should go on his head, because he would be a Nazirite dedicated to God and save Israel from the Philistines (Judges 13:2–25). This narrative in which the angel appears to give a promise of progeny to Manoah's wife shows contrast with other stories involving barren women who initiate contact with the divine to plead for fertility.

The woman runs to tell her husband about her theophany. Manoah does not question his wife's encounter but would like the messenger to provide more explicit instructions. He prays for the man of God to return and give them guidelines on how to care for their future son (13:2). Much to Manoah's frustration, however, the messenger of God, when he does reappear, merely repeats the dietary restrictions, adding only, "let the woman observe all I told her." The messenger in effect reasserts his confidence in the woman's power to carry out the mission. The rabbinic commentary *Midrash Rabba* to Numbers focuses on why the angel addressed the woman first, concluding that she must have been an unusually righteous person.[4] Modern commentators tend to stress the contrast drawn in the biblical narrative between the wife and the husband: "The story makes Manoah look foolish, but his wife appears wise," says Bellis.[5] While Manoah could be commended for his concern regarding the child's upbringing, his wife is notably given the greater responsibility in the vision.

When the woman bears a son and becomes a mother, she names him Samson (13:24). But unlike other mothers in the Bible, this mother does not explain the significance of the name. It has been suggested that the Hebrew root *sh-m-sh*, can be understood as a diminutive form of the noun *shemesh* ("sun") so that *Shimson* means: "little sun."[6] Various features of Samson's story suggest a connection with solar motifs such as the mention of Beth-Shemesh, "house of the sun," which was a short distance from the Sorek Valley, his birthplace. Did his mother give the name to him because she anticipated his heroic strength and miraculous energy? If so, he sadly dashed his mother's hopes when he met his nemesis in the woman, Delilah, whose name sounds like the Hebrew for "night" and "darkness." In presenting characters of these names, the text purposely seems to be juxtaposing light and dark, in order to foreshadow the evil that would eventually overtake Samson. As noted in his insightful article on Samson, Crenshaw points out that there are many such juxtapositions in the text,[7] which further strengthen our idea about the names of Samson and Delilah. Even in its style the account of Samson delights in textual tension, in order to emphasize the joys and sorrows that overtake the various players in the story.

Unlike Samson and Delilah, Samson's mother is unnamed in the text. The Talmud later gives her the name Hazelponi, for having turned her face (*ponah*) to behold the angel, so marking her encounter with the angel as the signal event of her life.[8] Whereas the rabbis felt the need to name the unnamed woman, one modern commentator argues that her namelessness is not necessarily a sign of powerlessness and in fact works to strengthen the motifs of the story.[9] Although names generally carry enormous significance in ancient Israel, it is the very namelessness of the mother in this text that occupies the most importance. She has an encounter with the angel, and hers is a far superior and more meaningful one than that of her husband. Her namelessness allows the reader to mentally attach her with the angelic figure,[10] who issues special instructions for Samson's upbringing and additionally requires Samson's mother to uphold a similar standard in her own life. After informing her that she will bear a child, the angel warns the woman, "Now be careful not to drink wine or other intoxicant, or to eat anything unclean"(Judg.13:4). Samson's mother, then, is foreshadowed in the story as having a more significant role than her husband in the spiritual life and godly rearing of her son.

Although beginning auspiciously, Samson's life takes a sad turn. The joy Samson's mother initially must have experienced at the prophetic birth of her gifted son turns to grave disappointment. As Fewell notes, Samson's mother "knows that the future is conditional (upon obedience to Nazirite law) and limited (Samson will only *begin* to deliver Israel from the Philistine oppression)."[11] To my knowledge, Mieke Bal is the only other commentator, ancient or modern, to track the story of this woman to its bitter end, as Samson's mother loses her influence on Samson. Bal concludes that Samson spent his life trying to escape his mother, but she begs the provocative question of whether the commands of his mother can and should be conflated with the commands of God.[12] One can speculate that she endeavored to impress upon her son the importance of his status and responsibility as a Nazirite, whose life is dedicated to God. For mothers were not only physical nurturers but also cultural and spiritual educators of their children.[13] We might imagine that she directed Samson to lead a holy life, and therefore his first action as an adult is not only personally disappointing but appears socially deviant as well. Samson asks his mother and father to get him a Philistine woman for a wife. His parents unhappily indulge his wishes, which, paradoxically, are supported by God as a pretext to initiate a conflict between the Israelites and the Philistines. In other words, the biblical narrator explains Samson's marriage to a Philistine woman as part of God's plan to destroy the Philistines who had dominion over Israel at that time (Judges 14: 4).

Samson's exploits against the Philistines occasioned his erotic involvement with three different women.[14] His first wife was the Philistine woman from Timnah mentioned above. His second involvement was with a harlot from Gaza. It was the third woman, Delilah, who engineered Samson's downfall, delivering the fatal blow to his mother's ambition. Putting Samson at risk on three different occasions, Delilah ruthlessly seeks to discover the secret to his power. Her final attempt appeals to his heart, attacking the sincerity of his love. She plaintively asks, "How can you say you love me when you don't confide in me?" (Judges 15:15). Her persistent nagging and accusations beat him into a confession. Under the weight of his passion and Delilah's intrigue, Samson regresses from the heroic to the henpecked. He divulges the secret of his strength as stemming from his status as a *nazir*, promised to the service of God "since his mother's womb" (Judges16: 17). The image of the mother's womb further associates Samson the invulnerable man with Samson the helpless infant. Not only does he reveal the secret known only to himself and his mother, but he naively trusts Delilah as a child might put trust in his mother.[15] In fact, Delilah almost emerges as a surrogate mother, albeit, an incompetent and evil one.

The imagery of the womb recalls the circumstances around Samson's birth and thus of his national mission. We are reminded of his childhood where his mother's pious influence and aspirations ultimately come to naught. That this history is recalled in the moment of his downfall brings his relationship with his family and especially with his mother, into focus. We see in one recriminating moment the defeat of a mother's hope for her son.[16]

The Samson narrative juxtaposes an ideal Israelite mother with three foreign women. Samson's life began with the godly influence of his religious mother, but unfortunately ended after his devastating encounters with three foreign women. The Hebrew words *yarad*, "to go down," and *alah*, "to go up," feature prominently in Samson's story giving the words symbolic importance. His life was indeed filled with many ups and downs. The life of Samson and his parents begins with a holy flame of the angel ascending, but eventually his life was a tragic *yerida,* a "downfall." Though his Hebrew name Shimshon means "sun-man," his life was not lived in the light of the sun, but in the shadow of lust.

Although his mother had high hopes for his spiritual development, his life ultimately we speculate was a great frustration to his parents. His story is a tragic one in the pages of biblical history. Further, he remains the sole example within the Bible of the evil that can result when one does not heed his mother's advice. Although Samson's mother was successful in following the commands issued to her during her pregnancy, Samson falls short of his obligations. In this text, it is the Israelite woman and mother who is the righteous and pious follower of God; Samson chooses to give into his baser urges, sexually pursuing outside dalliances.

He again and again rebels against God, but in the final scene of the story he cries out to the deity in desperation, hoping for one last chance to show his strength. He calls out, "O Lord God, please remember me, and give me strength just this once, O God, to take revenge upon the Philistines, if only for one of my two eyes!" (Jud.16:28). The pathos of this moment is overwhelming. Samson, whose birth was a promise to greatness, was living out his final days enslaved by the Philistines. He prayed for one last moment of glory to live up to his namesake and God answered his request—the pagan temple came crashing down, killing a large number of Philistines. Perhaps his religious upbringing and the influence of his devout mother played into God's merciful intervention in the final days of his life.

His story provides an interesting foil to the ones found in Genesis. While Genesis is rife with illustrations of devoted mothers who raise sons dedicated to living within the covenant and given tradition, here we are presented with a faithful mother whose godly influence sadly had little impact on the course of her son's life.

HANNAH

Our first encounter with Hannah presents a woman distraught over her childlessness, similar to situations we witnessed in earlier narratives of the matriarchs Sarah, Rebecca, and Rachel. Hannah's sadness and sense of emptiness cannot be appeased even by her husband's rhetorical question: "Am I not more to you than ten sons?" (1 Sam.1:8). However not even a husband's loving attention can appease Hannah's emptiness—only motherhood can alleviate her sorrow.[17] Hannah's story was, of course, intended to be viewed in the framework of the book of Samuel, as background for the miraculous birth and life of a great Israelite leader. Yet her powerful determination to overcome adversity places her at the forefront of the compelling narrative.

Hannah goes up with her family to the yearly sacrifice at the shrine at Shiloh (a detail that incidentally provides scriptural evidence that women did attend these places of worship).[18] Because of her sorrow regarding her barrenness, she weeps and declines to eat the sacrificial meal, and at its conclusion, goes to the sanctuary. This behavior is unique to Hannah, as the earlier matriarchs did not personally turn to prayer as a way to overcome their barrenness. She proactively seeks a solution to her infertility. Hannah appeals directly to God for a son:

> . . . she prayed to the LORD, weeping all the while. And she made this vow: . . . if You will grant Your maidservant a male child, I will dedicate him to the LORD for all the days of his life; and no razor shall ever touch his head.' (1Sam.1:11)[19]

Hannah's desire for a child is so desperate that she is willing to wholly dedicate him to the service of God. This distinguishes her from her barren predecessors. While they receive instruction from an angel as to how they should raise the child they would miraculously bear, Hannah imposes righteous standards upon herself and her offspring. In this way, she emerges as a strong, assertive and determined barren women who dares to challenge destiny. She daringly enters the sanctuary and plaintively beseeches God for a child, assuring him of her devotion to raise a son in a godly manner and to dedicate him to lifelong service in the tabernacle.

As Eli watches Hannah's emotional plea, he notices that her lips move, yet her voice is silent. Mistakenly, he believes her to be drunk. Yet, Hannah replies sincerely:

> Oh no, my lord! I am a very unhappy woman. I have drunk no wine or other strong drink, but I have been pouring out my heart to the LORD. Do not take your maidservant for a worthless woman; I have only been speaking all this time out of my great anguish and distress (1Sam.1:14–15).

Eli takes pity and blesses her, saying, "go in peace," and "may the God of Israel grant what you have asked of him." Thus reassured, and in an optimistic frame of mind, confident that she will soon experience motherhood, she goes on her way.

During the next year Hannah bears a son whom she names Samuel. Her naming speech is noteworthy: "And she called his name Samuel, for [she] asked him from the LORD." This initial naming speech gives etiological[20] justification for Samuel's given name. Further, it connects his name with the root *sh-'-l*, a root that figures largely in the Hebrew narrative, occurring numerous times in describing his life. Later, when elaborating on Samuel's name, Hannah emphasizes her own experience concerning his birth and destiny, stating, "I am the woman who stood beside you and prayed to the Lord; it was this child I prayed for, and the Lord granted what I asked from him. For as long as he lives, he is lent to the Lord" (1 Sam.1:26–28). So the great prophet Samuel is both "asked for," and then "lent to," as reflected in his name.

Since Hannah has made a vow to dedicate her son to God, she must give Samuel (Shmuel) up after he is weaned. Until that time, Hannah tells her husband that she will not accompany him on their annual trips to the tabernacle in Shiloh. She refuses to leave Samuel alone, devotedly immersed in the demands of infant care and savoring the brief period she will have with her son. When the time arrives that Samuel is weaned, Hannah dresses him and takes him to the sanctuary. Knowing that her son would remain in the tabernacle for good, Hannah must have put off the day of parting. Even though Samuel no longer lived under her roof, Hannah watched her son's growth from afar. From that time on, Hannah regularly sews a robe for Samuel to wear along with his priestly vestments and would present it to him when she would come to visit at Shiloh on the family's annual pilgrimage (I Sam. 2:19). Elsewhere, the Bible records the Israelite custom of giving a special gift to a favored child. This custom appears in Jacob's gift to Joseph. Hannah continues this tradition by literally weaving her maternal love into the daily religious existence of her first-born son. This act alone demonstrates Hannah's continued love and presumed influence in Samuel's life. The success of Samuel's career should attest to the truth of his mother's influence.

We here learn from Hannah's experience as well as Samson's mother's, that mothers at that time had the power to dedicate their sons to holy service. There is no evidence of a father or anyone else contradicting Hannah's initial dedication to temple service. I argue therefore that the vow of the mother has legal force and society's approval. I credit Hannah with having educated and molded Samuel's character in the brief period that he spent with her and, subsequently, through her yearly visits. By dint of her dedication and influence, Hannah carves for her son a place in the history of the Hebrew nation. Indeed

Samuel is credited with being one of the greatest Israelite leaders and with an ability to pray comparable to that of Moses.[21] From the moment of conception, and even in cases prior to conception, a mother's influence on her son's development is decisive. This influence demonstrates the power if not the authority of biblical women.

Perhaps we can also comment on Hannah's name, which comes from the root *h-n-n*, and has two possible meanings. The primary meaning of this root is "to be gracious" or "to show favor." Her name then reflects the eventual blessing of fertility that she receives from God. God shows favor to her and grants her request. The secondary meaning of the same root is "to be loathsome." This meaning may have been hinted at in the initial treatment Hannah received from her co-wife, Peninnah, who mocks Hannah for her barrenness. The two meanings inherent within Hannah's name speak to her experience: first she is loathsome, then she receives favor from God. Her name also speaks to her own character in raising her son. She is gracious and kind in her mothering, making great sacrifices for his sake. Although she desperately wants to bear a child, she agrees to give him up to religious service.

Hannah's second prayer found in 1 Samuel 2 is an interesting appendage to the story. Instead of being an elaboration of Hannah's childlessness and eventual fecundity, the poem praises God's power and ability to reverse human fortune. The way in which the song generalizes the change in fortune experienced by the speaker of the prayer makes her text applicable to others who have come into contact with God's grace and intervention. The following verses mention motherhood and are relevant to our topic:

> Those once sated must hire out for bread;
> Those once hungry hunger no more.
> While the barren woman bears seven,
> The mother of many is forlorn.
> ... The LORD makes poor and makes rich.
> He casts down, He also lifts high.
>
> (1 Samuel 2:5,7)

Although many commentators view the prayer as a later addition, it is significant that it is included here and attributed to Hannah. Tradition assumes that the prayer uttered in the first chapter can be read in conjunction with the second. In her prayer Hannah recognizes God's sovereignty over every area of life, particularly the area of parenthood.

Before leaving the mother figure of Hannah, we must mention that her manner of prayer has greatly impressed later Jewish tradition. The rabbis make much of her posture of prayer.[22] They use Hannah's prayer as a model for both men and women on how one should correctly petition God. The moving of her lips and simultaneous silence gives direction, the rabbis believe for how a person ought to pray. The fact that Hannah's prayer was carefully handed down and then used to instruct future communities shows that her influence was widely felt. She is viewed as a Mother of Prayer, instructing the faithful on how to request God's favor.

THE SHUNAMMITE WOMAN

Whereas the stories about barren women revolve around their desires to have children, the Shunammite woman does not invest any of her identity in being a mother. She is introduced into the story as "a great woman," *ishah gedolah* (2 Kings 4:8).[23] Whether this is an honorific or merely a description is not clear. But her actions bespeak her independence, wealth and influence, which make her worthy of this epithet. To her credit, she is also a woman of great faith and wisdom. The text does not give her a name, but calls her the Shunammite, in reference to her place of birth and residence. She hails from Shunem, a small town in the north of Israel.

In contrast to the other barren women, the text suggests that the Shunammite never initiates discussion on the problem of barrenness, nor prays to be released of it, nor asks anyone else to put in supplications for her. The prophet Elisha asks his disciple how he show gratitude to the Shunammite, and Gehazi tells him of her barrenness. The text here presents us with the unique case of a woman who seems at first glace unbothered by her infertile state.

When Elisha visits her town, the Shunammite woman recognizes his aura of sanctity and identifies him as a man of God. She shows outstanding hospitality toward him. She feeds him, and prepares a room for him, furnishing it with a bed, table, stool and candlestick. This care she provides for Elisha foreshadows the later mothering role she will assume. The prophet wishes to reciprocate her generosity and offers to speak to the king or the army commander on her behalf (2 Kings 4:8–37). Expressing her independence and self-sufficiency, she replies, "I dwell among my own people" (2Kings 4:13), implying that she is content, capable, and not looking for honor or favors from him. Elisha's disciple Gehazi later volunteers the information that she is childless and her husband is old. Elisha, the prophet, known in the Bible for performing miracles, promises the Shunammite a child. Like Sarah, she reacts incredulously to his pledge, "Do not deceive me, man of God" (2 Kings 4:16), but does not issue the relieved and grateful response that one hears from the likes of Hannah. Had the Shunammite been barren so long and was her husband so old that she no longer wished to be reminded of her lost hopes? Had she never hoped for a child? Was she so successful in her privileged social position that she did not feel the desire or need for children? The text does not say, or even hint at an answer. Elisha nevertheless prophesies that the barren Shunammite woman who had given him hospitality would definitely bear a child. The prophecy is fulfilled, and she does bear a son, but her child soon dies. For the Shunammite to have gained a child and suddenly lose him, was simply too agonizing to endure. The Shunammite, now distraught, comes to Elisha begging him to revive her child, and reminding him that initially she had not even asked for this child. The prophet, sensing her pain, quickly commands Gehazi to run ahead to Shunem where he was to lay the prophet's staff on the child, perhaps a symbol of the authority to prevent any burial before the prophet arrives. Elisha returns with her to her home, attends to the boy, prays to God, and the child is miraculously revived (2 Kings 4:34–37).

The Shunammite is clearly a strong and capable woman. Her competence is demonstrated once again when she leaves her property and possessions to travel to Phoenicia for the well-being of her son during the famine. We note the absence of the mention of the father during this period and consider the strength in the Shunammite's actions as a single parent.

The Shunammite woman, initially indifferent and skeptical of the idea of having a child, nevertheless devotes herself heart and soul to the care of her son once he is born. The father is not involved during the illness of the son (2 Kings 4:19). Although not following the prototype of previously discussed barren women, the Shunammite woman nevertheless does display the same fierce devotion to and protectiveness of her son's life that is evident throughout the mother stories of the Bible.

This story of Elisha and the Shunammite woman is a unique one in the Hebrew Bible. The story opens with a woman who seemingly has no need of, or desire for a family. She is independent and self-sufficient, even to the point of evading and ignoring the prophet's suggestion that she might want to bear a child. However, once she experiences the joys of motherhood she finds herself engrossed in the experience of parenting her son. The Shunammite woman then joins with her biblical counterparts in earnestly (and perhaps even aggressively) pursuing the welfare of her boy, even without the assistance of her husband. She is a particularly strong figure in that she dominates the narrative and her story demonstrates that women could find power through their role as mother.

THE MOTHER OF JABEZ

The story of Jabez (1Chr.4:9–10) invites inclusion in the book because it deals with both a mother and a child's given name. We have mentioned the tendency in the biblical world to play on names in the stories of Genesis and also in the stories included in the early historical books. The potent force of a name, particularly when given by a mother, is especially highlighted in the story of Jabez, whose name could be associated with the Hebrew word for "distress." His given name seems to urge him to seek God for deliverance of some unforeseeable evil.

The brief story told in 1 Chronicles is worth relating.

> "Jabez was more honored than his brothers; and his mother named him Jabez, 'Because,' she said, 'I bore him in pain.' Jabez invoked the God of Israel, saying, 'Oh, bless me, enlarge my territory, stand by me, and make me not suffer pain from misfortune!' And God granted what he asked" (1 Chronicles 4: 9–10).[24]

The name Jabez appears here not on a genealogical list but as an etiology. Though the text praises Jabez for being more honorable than his brothers, nevertheless his mother names him Jabez because "[She] bore him in pain." Jabez, whose root consonants are '-b-s signifies a reversal of the root letters of '-s-b, which means "sorrow."[25] We suggest in the context of the story that the mother may have intentionally switched the letters in a superstitious move to actually ward off any pain that might threaten her son.[26]

As an adult, Jabez calls out to God and asks to be blessed. Why does he ask for a blessing? The text is ambiguous, but we can conjecture that living with the stigma of his unfortunate name proved too difficult. Did Jabez grow up hearing over and over again that he was named for his mother's pain at his birth? Even though his mother changed the consonants around, Jabez apparently did not understand the root change as a defensive switch. To the contrary his name may have frightened him for the fate it seemed to announce, and it prompts him to cry to God for blessing.[27] Somewhat surprisingly God gives him what he requests. The man Jabez prospers. Jabez's story begins as an etiology and develops into a reversal of (anticipated) fortune or misfortune, as the case may be.

This story has special significance for the topic at hand for it demonstrates how much influence a mother may have in the destiny of her child. Though Jabez's life is not fraught with the suffering and hardship one might expect from one of his namesake, his name, given by his mother, greatly influences later life decisions. He struggles with fear of misfortune that hovers over his subconscious for the course of his life. This story offers evidence that women, as mothers, could assign names—an act of power in ancient Israel. Further, this tale of triumph and tragedy underscores the power that a mother can have on the life of her offspring.

MOTHERS IN NEGATIVE ROLES

Up to this point, we have concentrated on mothers who present positive role models. The following examples point out that not all mothers in the historical books attained these standards. Even though the following examples are negative, the women nevertheless deserve attention here because of their role as "mother," and the influence, whether good or bad, they exert over the lives of their sons. Mothers who do not fit the righteous mold are given scant attention by the ancient, medieval, and modern commentators. We explore the relevant passages to paint a more complete portrait of the mother.

Often these mothers are the witting or unwitting roots of evil that come upon their sons. In Judges 5, Sisera's mother virtually gloats over the likelihood that her son, if victorious, would rightfully ravage the enemy women. This leads Athalya Brenner to characterize her as "unsympathetic to other mothers or to women in general."[28] Pseudo-Philo names her Themech, "she who must be destroyed."[29] Sisera's mother, however, presents us with the only biological mother in the Song of Deborah. The poem in Judges preserves her true heart and intent to cause pain. She is mentioned here because she stands as an influential mothering figure, albeit, a negative one, in biblical tradition.

Over the ages, commentators have noted that the fates of Abimelech and Jephthah are shaped by the irregular marital status of their mothers.[30] Abimelech is the son of a concubine. Based on his family relationship, he eventually organizes his mother's family in a coup against the ruling seventy sons of his father (Judges 8:29–9:57). Jephthah's mother is a harlot (Judges 10:6–12:7). Because of his mother, his half brothers claim he is an outsider and disinherit him. This discrimination leads Jephthah to flee to another city where he settles among a group of unseemly characters. In their company, Jephthah develops into a ruffian. The above-mentioned men are connected by the fact that their mothers are figures of ill repute. Both Abimelech and Jephthah, we may speculate, were raised without the edifying influence of a godly mother and their lives show a lack of good mothering.

Another example of poor parentage is found in the figure Micah (Judg.17:1). The relationship between Micah, a man from the hill country of Ephraim, and his mother prompts some interesting speculations. Apparently Micah steals 1,100 shekels worth of silver from his mother. Upon realizing the theft, the mother curses whoever it was that stole from her. Micah overhears the curse and, apparently shaken up by it, returns the money. His mother gratefully exonerates him and then directly proceeds to invest part of the ransomed money in idols for her son to worship. The story reads as if she were rewarding him the seed money for a start-up business of questionable morals and indeed it seems that Micah wishes to establish his own cultic shrine. Although the biblical text paints the mother negatively, the story also shows a woman and mother as a major participant in household religious activities.

Though we focus here on the role of the mother in the historical books, the Bible provides us with other examples of somewhat debased mothers. The book of Kings, for example, shows the perversion of the instinctive protectiveness of mothers in situations of extreme hardship. During the great famine in Samaria, two mothers are found desperately wanting for food. One suggests to the other that they first eat one of their sons and then eat the other. "So we cooked my son and we ate him" (2 Kings 6:29). Once the king gets word of this perversion, he tears his clothes and mourns (2 Kings 6:30). One imagines that the king is repulsed by this instance of cannibalism and is subsequently motivated to seek a solution to the plight of war that ostensibly drives these mothers to such desperation (II Kings 6:24–30).

A similar horror is described in Lamentations: "The hands of women full of compassion have cooked their own children; such become their food, in the destruction of the daughter of my people" (Lam.4:10; see also Lam.2: 20: Jer. 19:9). The harshness of their history drives mothers in these stories to act against their own human instincts. The mothers here are depicted not as good or wise but as sadly reduced to betraying feelings of compassion for their offspring.

These folktales of cannibalism are mind-numbingly horrific. The awfulness of the stories lead us to believe that the narrator intends his readers to reflect on the utter moral collapse of society. The narrator uses mother figures to play on reader expectations and to comment on the social disorder. Society, according to the narrator, had completely disintegrated to the point that predictable maternal instinct could not be relied upon for evidence of social compassion.

SUMMARY OF THE MOTHERS OF A BUDDING NATION

This chapter primarily focused on four significant mothers, Samson's mother, Hannah, the Shunammite, and the mother of Jabez. We also briefly looked the so-called negative mothers of ancient Israel. By studying these women we hope to have shed light on how mothers helped to shape the destiny of their children, many of whom eventually developed into powerful figures in the landscape of Israel's history. These women mothered at a chaotic time in Israel's history, during the transitional period between the rule of judges and the reign of kings. The Israelite people were coming into nationhood and the mothers we discussed played a large role in the development of a loose confederation of tribes into a structured autonomous nation. They produced the leaders that fashioned the destiny of a nation.

Barrenness figures largely as a theme in our discussion. Hannah's longing for a child is almost as passionate as those of the matriarchs, while Samson's mother does not actively pine for a son. The Shunamite woman outright rejects the notion of having a child and appears fulfilled without being a mother. Lastly, we look at mothers who possess authority, but to whom we attribute a negative maternal influence.

The range of difference between all these women shows a divergence with the women discussed in the chapter on the mothers of Genesis. While the mothers of Genesis were mothers of tribes, these mothers are presented as living in the land of Canaan after the conquest. The mothers of this chapter are mothers of a budding nation. The tribal network presented in Genesis has grown into a confederation of lands governed by judges. New concerns inform the behavior of these mothers. They are not only consumed with bearing children, but are also engaged with shaping destinies of heroic leaders. The social and political concerns of a burgeoning nation influence their decisions and behavior. As we move on, we will encounter women, the wise women and queen mothers of the following chapter, who are far more involved in molding the nation.

NOTES

1. Finding the appropriate heading for these books proves challenging. The books of Judges, Samuel, and Kings that are discussed in this chapter are also considered prophetic histories and Former Prophets as well as literary texts.

2. Mary Calloway, *Sing, O Barren One, A Study in Comparative Midrash* (Atlanta: Scholar's Press, 1986), 32.

3. Calloway, 32.

4. *Numbers Rab.* 10:5.

5. Alice Ogden Bellis, *Helpmates, Harlots, and Heroes* (Kentucky: Westminster/John Knox Press, 1994), 123. Similar points are made by J. L. Crenshaw, *Samson: A Secret Betrayed, A Vow Ignored* (Atlanta, Georgia: John Knox, 1978); J. Cheryl Exum, "Promise and Fulfillment: Narrative Art in Judges 13," *Journal of Biblical Literature*, 99 (1980); 43–59; Alice Laffey, *An Introduction to the Old Testament: A Feminist Perspective* (Philadelphia, Pennsylvania: Fortress Press, 1988); and J.A. Soggin, *Judges: A Commentary*, trans. J.S. Bowden (Philadelphia, Pennsylvania: Westminster Press, 1981).

6. J.Crenshaw, "Samson," in the *Anchor Bible Dictionary* Vol. 5 (New York: Doubleday, 1992), 950

7. Crenshaw, 953.

8. *Numbers Rab.* 10:5, 11:7. See also *Yalqut Shimoni* on Judges 13 and b. *Baba Bathra* 91a. The name *Hazelponi* occurs in 1 Chronicles 4:3 but is given to Samson's mother in *Numbers Rab.* 10:5 and in b.*Baba Bathra* 91a. Pseudo-Philo says that her name was Eluma, daughter of Remac, but this name is found nowhere else in Jewish literature; See Daniel J. Harrington, "Pseudo-Philo's Biblical Antiquities," *The Old Testament Pseudepigrapha*, vol. 2, ed. James H. Charlesworth, (New York, New York: Doubleday & Co., 1985), Chapter 4, 356)

9. Adele Reinhartz, "Samson's Mother: An Unnamed Protagonist," in *A Feminist Companion to Judges*, ed. Athalya Brenner (Sheffield, England: Sheffield Academic Press, 1993), 169.

10. Reinhartz, 168

11. Donna Nolan Fewell, "Judges," in *The Woman's Bible Commentary*, eds. by Carol Newsom and Cheryl Ringe (Louisville: Westeminster/John Knox Press, 1992), 76.

12. Mieke Bal, *Death & Dissymmetry* (Chicago, Illinois: University of Chicago Press, 1988), 201.

13. Carol Meyers, *Discovering Eve* (New York, New York: Oxford University Press, 1988), 150.

14. The woman from Timnah who becomes his wife eventually meets a terrible death because of a series of vengeful reprisals between Samson and the Philistines. His second liaison is a harlot from Gaza. This entanglement led to an ambush of Samson by the citizens of Gaza, but Samson proved his strength and escaped.

15. Mieke Bal, *Op. Cit.,* 202.

16. Danna Nolan Fewell, *Op. Cit.*, 73–4.

17. See Genesis 30:1 for a similar situation of a barren woman's interactions with her husband. See Yairah Amit's article "Am I Not More Devoted To You Than Ten Sons?" in *A Feminist Companion to Samuel and Kings*, ed. Athalya Brenner (Sheffield, England: Sheffield Academic Press, 1994), 26–42. See also Nehama Aschkenasy, *Eve's Journey* (Detroit, Michigan: Wayne State University Press, 1986), 77ff.

18. Although the topic of female religious participation is outside the scope of this book, the fact that Hannah attended worship services alongside her family is significant, showing that women did participate in the ancient cultus in Israel. For more on this topic, see, I. J. Peritz, "Women in the Ancient Hebrew Cult," *JBL* 17 (1898) 114, 129–30; C.J. Vos, *Women in Old Testament Worship* (Delft: Judels and Brinkman, 1968), 60ff.

19. Hannah intended him to become a Nazarite, devoted to the service of God. Interestingly, she makes a vow and does not need or ask for her husband's consent. A similar detail is seen in the story of Samson, whose mother dedicates her son to Nazariteship (Judges 13). Mishnah Nazir 4:6 later forbids this practice.

20. An etiology is a story which explains the meaning of something, while an etymology refers to the grammatical explanation.

21. See Psalm 99:6 and Jeremiah 15:1.

22. y.Ber. 4,1; translated in the *Talmud of the Land of Israel*, vol.1, *Berachot*, trans.Tzvee Zahavy, ed.J. Neusner (Chicago: The University of Chicago Press, 1989), 149; cf. b.Ber. 31a-b. Yom. 73a-b. See also my article, "Hannah's Prayer: Rabbinic Ambivalence," *Shofar* 17, no. 2 (1999): 36–48.

23. *Isha gadolah* seems to be a descriptive here, but also may function as an honorific. If it were being used as a title, then one might expect to find its employment elsewhere.

24. Later Hebrew tradition takes the praise not the curse that Jabez was more honorable than all his brothers, and identifies him as the Judge Othniel cited in b.Temurah 16a in the Book of Judges many times and in 1Chronicles 4:13.

25. The root '-b-s is used neither in Hebrew nor Aramaic. Probably it is an Amorite verb which corresponds to the Hebrew root '-s-b. See "Jabez," *Anchor Bible Dictionary*, vol. 3, (New York: Doubleday, 1992), 595.

26. See Sara Japhet, *I & II Chronicles* (Louisville, Kentucky: Westminster/John Knox Press, 1993) for more commentary on the name "Jabez."

27. See Jacob who changes his son's name from "son of my pain" given by Rachel to son of my right hand (Genesis 35:18).

28. Athalya Brenner, "A Triangle and a Rhombus in Narrative Structure: A Proposed Integrative Reading of Judges 4 and 5," in *A Feminist Companion to Judges*, ed. Athalya Brenner (Sheffield, England: Sheffield Academic Press, 1993) 102.

29. See above, Harrington, "Pseudo-Philo" 31:8, 345.

30. Ginzburg (1946), vol. 4, 43, *Mik'roat Gedolot* on Judges 11:1–2.

Chapter Three

Wise Women and Queen Mothers

My son . . . do not forsake the instruction of your mother

Proverbs 1:8

He had a throne placed for the Queen mother, and she sat on his right.

1 Kings 2:19

God could not be everywhere and therefore he made mothers.

UNKNOWN. A Jewish Proverb

The wise women and queen mothers to be discussed here appear in different books in the Bible including the order they are to be analyzed: the Book of Proverbs, 2 Samuel, 1 & 2 Kings, and 1 & 2 Chronicles. The mothers in these books do not take after their foremothers whose universal and intense desire for children ruled their passions. These later figures occupy a level of motherhood that transcends the biological definition of childbearing and includes a wider scope of cultural and political influence. These accomplished women fulfill the roles of wives, mothers, and counselors who act as leaders not only in the private sector but to some degree in the public domain as well. Because wisdom plays a large role in how the queen mothers behave (and obviously in how the wise women operate), we start our study with a short analysis of the feminine personification of Wisdom in the book of Proverbs. The idealization of the sagacious mother figure presented in the book of Proverbs has great impact on how the wise women and queen mothers are presented in the historical books of Samuel, Kings and Chronicles. This idealized wise mother figure thus provides a connection between these two groups of women. After establishing this association, I then move on to analyze each of the wise women and queen mothers.

FEMININE PERSONIFICATION OF WISDOM

The book of Proverbs personifies Wisdom, *hokhmah*, as a woman (Prov. 1–9).[1] The term *hokhmah* in Hebrew is grammatically feminine. Reflecting the specific Israelite tradition, Wisdom in the Book of Proverbs begins and ends with the fear of God (Proverbs 1:7).[2] Wisdom is described as mother, prophet, beloved wife and partner, the first creation of God, and the source of all human knowledge and blessings of health, happiness and wealth to her followers. According to the biblical scholar, Claudia Camp, the exalted figure of female Wisdom coupled with the ideal of the woman of valor served as symbols to normalize an increasing balance of power between men and women in a time of "economic pressure, de-urbanization, and incipient democratization." She also demonstrates that the "wisdom of women often functions toward divine ends."[3] Her study of the meaning and values associated with the female wisdom figure helps us to understand the role played by the woman and mother in society. A person who doled out wisdom could obtain much clout, thus maternal figures who offered advice achieved a measure of influence in Israelite society.

The female personification of Wisdom serves not only as a symbol but also as a model for life. Throughout the book the figure of Wisdom, an abstraction that speaks as if it were a human being, calls on people to listen to her voice and hearken to her teachings: "Wisdom cries aloud in the street; in the markets she raises her voice" (Proverbs 1:20). The most highly praised mothers in scripture are those who heed Wisdom's cry. Later on in Proverbs, it is the wise woman who "builds her house" (9:1).

One of Wisdom's early teachings relates to how a child should honor his parents. "Listen my son to the instruction of your father, forget not the teaching of your mother" (Prov.1:8; 6:20). Wisdom resonates with the themes of Exodus 20:12, Leviticus 19:3, and Deuteronomy 5:16, providing us with a most vivid picture of the authority of mothers and their equality to fathers particularly in the education of their children from school age through adulthood. Interestingly, throughout the book of Proverbs many teachings are addressed to a "son" or "sons," from a father-teacher. However, the female personification of wisdom at times acts as a mother-teacher.[4]

The book of Proverbs has more to say about the respect and love due the mother than any other book in the Bible.[5] The most well known portion of the book is the praise, *Eshet Hayil*, the woman of valor. This poem presents a portrait of a woman who is manager, not only of her own household but also of business enterprises outside the home, which she conducts with efficiency and competence.

> She looks for wool and flax,
> And sets her hand to them with a will.
> She is like a merchant fleet, bringing her food from afar.
> She rises while it is still night,
> And supplies provisions for her household (Prov. 31:10 ff).

At the end of the song we hear how her husband, children, and elders sing her praises (Prov 31:28–9). Significantly, as Camp further notes, "it is difficult to read Proverbs' paeans to the power of both wisdom personified as a woman (chaps. 1–9) and of woman as the ideal representative of wisdom (chap. 31) without imagining some related social reality at their base." We imagine that mothers had achieved a known measure of social power so that the author of Proverbs naturally could turn to a female figure to exemplify ideal wisdom. Proverbs' depiction of Wisdom as a woman, and the woman as valorous, model positive roles for women that we will now study in the historical books of scripture.

WISE WOMEN

Before studying the prominent royal mothers, we want to investigate the wise women within non-royal masses. The following women stand out as both devoted mothers and sagacious counselors whose influence has far-reaching impact (2 Samuel 14:1–22 and 20:17–22). The two mothers discussed below are designated by the title "wise woman" (*'isha hakhamah*), and their advice perhaps reflects the influence of the wisdom literature of Proverbs.

The first wise woman appears in the story of Absalom, who murders his half-brother Amnon for raping his sister Tamar (2 Sam.13). Absalom fears a reprisal for his murder and escapes his father's court. Joab, commander-in-chief of David's army, senses David's desire to be reconciled with Absalom, so he contrives to restore Absalom to the court. In conceiving a plan, Joab enlists the help of a wise woman from the city of Tekoa, whose experience as a mother contributes to the aptness of her counsel. Joab brings the woman to the king. In the ensuing dialogue the woman describes the trouble between her own two sons that resulted in the one killing the other. Continuing with her narrative, she describes how the townsfolk were set upon condemning the murderer, which would leave the women bereft of both sons and her dead husband without an heir. "Let Your Majesty be mindful of the Lord your God and restrain the blood avenger bent on destruction, so that my son may not be killed" (2 Samuel 14:11). The woman succeeds in persuading the king to guard her remaining son's safety. She then masterfully turns her plea to the more general cause of reconciliation. This diplomatic turn brings the king to realize the injustice of his own son's exile and convinces him to order the high-minded, vengeful Absalom back (2 Sam 14). The successful bidding of the woman of Tekoa was in large part due to her own experience and compassion gained as a mother looking out for her family's best interests. Through her skillful maneuvering, the woman of Tekoa cleverly effected national change. The king responded to her parable concerning parents and children and reconciled with his son.

Another *'isha hakhamah* of the Bible, the wise woman of Abel, speaks out fearlessly when her city is threatened by Joab and his army (2 Samuel 20). With skillful oratory, this woman confronts Joab, who is standing outside the wall, and causes him to reflect. "I am one of those who seek the welfare of the faithful in Israel. But you seek to bring death upon a city and a mother in Israel![6] Why should you destroy the Lord's possession" (2 Sam.20:19)? She invokes the image of the mother in defending her city, suggesting that a mother—in this case, the city—is too sacred for such a violent attack. Just as a mother cares for her offspring, so a city looks after its denizens. This woman perhaps could be alluding to her own experience as a mother by speaking on behalf of the city's safety because she recognizes its likewise importance in nurturing its inhabitants. She sees that the destruction of the city would mean the end of much life, but also would destroy potential producers of progeny, in other words, the city's mothers. Influenced by the woman's words, Joab agrees to withdraw as long as he is allowed to take custody of a certain rebel. Hoping to save the entire city, the woman instructs the inhabitants, men and women alike, *behokhmatah* "in her wisdom" to locate and capture the named culprit (2 Sam 20:22). Her counsel is accepted and the city and its mothers (and potential mothers) are saved.

Ackerman makes the additional point that the woman's decisive and respected leadership earns her the honorific "mother in Israel" as well. She states, "If the city Abel-Beth-Ma'acah embodies what it means to be 'a mother in Israel' by using skills in persuasive counseling to protect 'the heritage of Yahweh,' then could one not argue—as was in fact assumed by the ancient midrashic tradition—that the wise woman who speaks for the city also deserves the 'mother in Israel' designation?[7] This certainly is an interesting point, but we will not delve into the use of "mother in Israel" as an honorific here. In our chapter on "Metaphorical Mothers" we address the phrase and develop the idea of woman who mothers on a large scale, giving counsel to a nation of symbolic children.

But who was this wise woman who successfully directs her people at a time of national emergency? There are three similar instances in biblical literature in which leaders negotiate at the city wall, but this is the only episode showing a woman as leader.[8] No information is offered in the Bible to explain how this woman acquired the education and skills needed to negotiate difficult political situations. As in the case of the story of the wise woman of Tekoa, we assume that she must have had some training for the sensitive political task she is shown carrying out with great wisdom.

While my main interest involves the wisdom that is conveyed through the image and context of the mother, sometimes mothers are used in examples to convey wisdom. While the following story ultimately highlights the wisdom of King Solomon, it also demonstrates how one mother acts wisely to save her child. This is the case of the two mothers who present their competing claim for a child to King Solomon.

> The king said, "One says, 'This is my son, the live one, and the dead one is yours'; and the other says, 'No, the dead boy is yours, mine is the live one.'" So the king gave the order, "Fetch me a sword." A sword was brought before the king, and the king said, "Cut the live child in two, and give half to one and half to the other." But the woman whose son was the live one pleaded with the king. . . ."Please, my lord," she cried, "give her the live child; only don't kill it!" (1 Kings 3:23–26).

In addition to confirming King Solomon's superior wisdom, this tale reveals a deeper quality relating to motherhood. It teaches that a wise mother, as shown here, would rather give up the claim to her child than sacrifice the child himself (I Kings 3:16–27). In other words, the essence of motherhood is self-sacrifice with an eye to securing the wellbeing and integrity of one's child, namely, acting with prudence. Up to this point in the story, the women are referred to as "harlots" or as "women." The title "mother" comes into play only after the true mother reveals herself through her selfless act stemming from her wisdom. "Give the live child to her, and do not put it to death; she is its mother," commands the king (I Kings 3:25). King Solomon recognizes the true mother through her sincere display of compassion. A mother's love knows no bounds, and in the words of Trible, "According to the story, the presence of a love that knows not the demands of ego, of possessiveness, or even of justice reveals motherhood."[9]

Another biblical story that illustrates a woman's self-sacrifice, but also her intelligence and her astute judgment is found in the story of Rizpah, daughter of Aiah. Like the previous example, this account presents another variation of a story about a mother's wisdom and self-sacrifice on behalf of her sons.[10] There is a famine in the land lasting three years. David is distraught and he inquires of God as to its cause (2 Sam. 1–3). He learns that the famine is due to Saul's massacre of the Gibeonites. The Gibeonites do not want monetary compensation but rather the death of Saul's descendants.

> They said: "The man who massacred us and planned to exterminate us, so that we should not survive in all the territory of Israel - let seven of his male issue be handed over to us, and we will impale them before God in Gibeah of Saul. . . .The king replied, "I will do so."

In the only reference to such strife between Saul and the Gibeonites in the Bible, King David surrenders to the Gibeonites King Saul's seven grandchildren: the five sons of Michal[11] and the two sons of Rizpah: Armoni and Mephiboshet. Rizpah, the royal concubine, could not prevent the sacrifice of her sons and relatives, but she carried out a vigil over their dead bodies so that no further dishonor would be done to their memory. It is reported that Rizpah kept away birds and animals of prey for five months, from mid-April to November. She took sackcloth, and spread it out to protect her by day and to rest on at night. The heat and rain and cold did not move her from watching over the corpses. Rizpah's courageous and prudent actions ultimately had sway over King David's decisions. When King David heard about Rizpah's love, courage and patience, he ordered that the sons and relatives be buried together with Saul and Jonathan. Though Rizpah had nothing to do with Saul's sin against the Gibeonites, she silently and alone had to bear the burden of the brutal loss of her sons. She, who as a concubine of a king, had worn royal robes, donned sackcloth for months in a unique story of a self-sacrificing and dedicated mother. She is included in our discussion on wise women because her prudence influenced the actions of a king.

QUEEN MOTHERS

Much like the wise women we discussed above the queen mothers' sphere of influence extends beyond the home to affect a larger sector of society. Their lives at court give them greater opportunity to observe the political, social, and religious activities in the land. They often establish alliances and influence dynastic decisions. In this section we discuss the nature of the queen mother's power and analyze specific examples of queen mothers to show this power in practice.

Queen mothers described in the Bible refer to the king's mother, not to his wife. It is significant that the phrase "and his mother was" appears twenty times in 2 Kings and 2 Chronicles. The frequent reference to the king's maternal line demonstrates the importance attributed to the queen mother. In the above-mentioned biblical books the text summarizes the king's achievement always stressing that "he did what was right in God's eyes" or "he did evil in the eyes of God." The juxtaposition of the queen mother's name with the evaluation of her son's rule points to the influence of her role in his life and at court. Some of these queen mothers are called *gevirah,* meaning "great lady" or "queen."[12] Scholars discuss the meaning of the title *gevirah* and debate whether the queen mother is accorded an official position in her own right or whether her power stems strictly from her biological relationship to her son, the king. I argue that they are powerful mothers not only by their womb but also by their wisdom.

A number of scholars, among them Ben-Barak, Andreasen, and Ackerman, have investigated the queen mother's position at the palace, and each offers a different theory to explain the queen mother's place and power at court. All three, however, see the roots of the institution of queen mother as being influenced by neighboring nations,[13] especially by the model of the Hittite queen who had important social, political, and cultic responsibilities at the Hittite court.[14] Perhaps we see the queen mother's power most positively modeled in the example of the Egyptian Pharoah Hatshepsut, a ruling queen and mother of the 16th century who built temples and took care of her people.[15] The queen mothers of ancient Israel do not possess the same level of power as their ancient Near Eastern counterparts, but they nonetheless, seem to hold similar positions.

In her study of queen mothers, Ben-Barak, claims that queen mothers do not hold an official position at court. She maintains that only very ambitious queen mothers use their influence to promote their son's ascension to the throne, and thereafter enhance their own power at court. Bathsheba, mother of King Solomon, to be discussed below, though not given the title *gevirah* clearly exemplifies Ben-Barak's approach.[16] In Ben-Barak's view, Bathsheba, though not in possession of an official title, wields influence by virtue of her personality and private ambition.

On the other hand, Andreasen argues that there is an official status for the *gevirah* in the kingdom.[17] He shows that the queen mother is treated with great deference by the king because she holds a significant official position superseded only by the king himself.[18] In contrast to Andreasen, Ackerman, suggests that the queen mother's influence is in the cultic arena rather than on the political scene.[19] As we discuss above, although biblical scholars are in disagreement about the exact nature of the queen mother's power, but they all concur that she does have some degree of authority. In sum these powerful female figures participated in a broad spectrum of activities, both political and social, and in some cases, are even involved in the religious arena. Below we will discuss the biblical references to queen mothers to determine their importance in Israelite life.

Perhaps one of the most telling proofs of the significance of queen mothers is the fact that they are named in the Bible. As we indicated above, the giving of a name often bestows identity and purpose upon an individual. Sadly many female characters of the Bible remain nameless, while males are usually mentioned by name. The naming factor in the queen mothers' stories forces us to take notice of them and elevates their status above the norm for either a man or a woman. Of the eighteen queen mothers whose names are listed, fifteen are mothers of Judean kings, two of Israelite kings, and one is from the period of the United Monarchy.[20] It is interesting to speculate why only two mothers of the many northern kings are named, while fifteen names of the mothers of Judean kings appear. The omission of the mothers' names from the northern kingdom could indicate that the institution of queen mother did not exist in Israel as this kingdom existed only for a short period and enjoyed little stability. There may not have been sufficient time to develop the institution of the queen mother in the north. The omission could also have been political because the biblical narrators regarded the rulers of the Northern Kingdom as wicked idol worshipers.

The Chronicles of the kings of Judah registered queen mothers. Those of the kings of Israel did not. Why record the names of mothers of evil rulers? One exception to this norm is Jeroboam. Jeroboam is considered the paradigm of sinfulness yet notwithstanding his notorious wickedness, his mother's name, Zeruah, is recorded. Jeroboam is continuously denounced in Kings not only as a sinner himself but for causing all Israel to sin (1 Kings 15:30). However, the tradition that Jeroboam was raised up by God as a foil to punish Solomon for his sins may explain why his mother's name is mentioned. In other words, the mention of Zeruah by name implies perhaps that she gave birth to a son who at the start of his rule achieved a divine purpose but who later went astray.

Perhaps a more convincing reason for omitting the queen mothers' names in Northern Israel, but naming those in Judah, may be an attempt to establish and defend the legitimacy of the Davidic dynasty's claim to rule over Israel. Every son had to have an identifiable mother to insure that he was a legitimate child, and each Judean queen mothers' name is always mentioned at the beginning of her son's reign. There are only two Judean kings' mothers who are not named: those of Jehoram and of Ahaz. Given the depth of evil attributed to these men, we might speculate that their mothers' anonymity is due to the kings' infamy. The Judean exception that proves the rule perhaps is Manasseh, the most evil king in Judah. The sources strongly denounce Manasseh yet his mother's name is listed (2 Kings 21:1). This explanation is in keeping with the above mentioned theory that the names of mothers of wicked kings are, for the most part, omitted, although this rule is not followed with complete consistency.

In sum, in most though not all cases, mothers of kings considered by the biblical narrator as good rulers were given the honor of being listed in the genealogy. It is not possible to explain convincingly why some of the mothers of wicked rulers are included and others excluded from the official record. Most likely the books of Kings and Chronicles include excerpts from different sources some of which included names of the mothers and some of which did not.[21]

Most of the queen mothers in the Israelite and Judean kingdoms are positive models of royalty. The archetype of the influential queen mother is best exemplified by Bathsheba, the mother of Solomon. She is informed by the prophet Nathan that an opposition party headed by Abiathar, the priest, and Joab, David's chief general, are supporting Adonijah to be crowned as king (1 Kings1–2). A strong force in the court party that included the prophet Nathan and the priest Zadok who supported Solomon as king, Bathsheba takes it upon herself to make a case to her husband on behalf of her son. In no uncertain terms, she reminds the king of his promise to appoint Solomon as his successor.

> My lord, you yourself swore to your maidservant by the LORD your God: 'Your son Solomon shall succeed me as king, and he shall sit upon my throne.' Yet now Adonijah has become king, and you, my lord the king, know nothing about it (1 Kings 1:17–8).

Bathsheba's active interest in her son's destiny contrasts with her earlier passivity as the young woman seduced by the indiscrete king. Whereas she has little power as a young woman manipulated by a commanding monarch, she achieves a much larger measure of control as a queen mother. As King David lay on his deathbed, Bathsheba is quick to advocate her son's right of succession and courageously confronts a difficult situation. David, who had been unaware of the intrigue at court, is moved by her entreaty and states: "As the Lord lives, who has redeemed my soul out of all distress, surely Solomon your son shall reign after me" (1 Kings1:29–30). At David's command Solomon is quickly anointed king by the priest Zadok. Although Bathsheba probably is motivated by her personal concern for Solomon's position, she likely also has the national welfare at heart. Securing King Solomon in the throne would avert a national political crisis in the unstable period of a transition government.

Solomon's relationship with his mother Bathsheba can be described as one of love and respect. We see Bathsheba enter a room to speak with her son, now the king. Solomon rises to greet her, bows, and asks that a seat be placed for her to the right of his throne. Each of these gestures signals respect. That Solomon places his mother on the right side, the side known to symbolize power and authority, confers onto her a certain authoritative status. When referencing her, he speaks of her in the third person as "the king's mother," which also accentuates her relation to royalty.

Further attesting to Bathsheba's royal standing in the court, Adonijah, Solomon's older half-brother, appeals to her to ask Solomon to allow him to marry Abishag, David's young concubine. When she appears before him with her request, Solomon says to her "Ask, my mother, for I will not say no to you" (1 Kings 2:20–21). But when he hears her request on behalf of his half-brother he explains to her Adonijah's treacherous motives. According to ancient Semitic custom the man who inherited the wives or concubines of the dead king would succeed to the crown. King Solomon refuses the request on the grounds that what she asked was equal to demanding the throne for his half-brother.[22]

How, one wonders, could Bathsheba be persuaded by Adonijah to bring his request before the king? The text suggests that she suspects his motives since she questions him about his intentions, but is persuaded that he is sincere in his love for his father's concubine Abishag, and is not plotting a revolt against his half-brother Solomon (1 Kings 2:13–18). Is she unaware of the threat this marriage might present to her son, the king? Might Solomon have suspected that his mother is plotting against him? Or is she in fact covertly conspiring against Adonijah, participating in a plot to destroy Adonijah to which Solomon would have been a knowing collaborator? If the plan is to kill Adonijah, it was successful. We can assume then that Bathsheba is acting in accordance with Solomon's best interests in mind, and further, demonstrating her wisdom in subtly manipulating the political circumstances. Solomon has him executed. What the meeting between mother and son reveals is that the queen mother's voice is an authoritative one to be seriously reckoned with.

The relationship between Solomon and Bathsheba is so influential within the tradition that later commentators identify unknown biblical personages with them. One such example occurs in the Book of Proverbs. A self-contained passage describes an unnamed queen mother who instructs an unknown King Lemuel on how a monarch is to behave:

> The words of Lemuel, King of Massa,
> With a moral teaching his mother corrected him…
> O my son, the son of my womb,
> Know, o son of my vows,
> Give not thy strength unto women,
> Nor thy ways to that which destroys kings.
> Wine is not for kings, O Lemuel,
> Not for kings to drink, nor any strong drink for princes
> Lest they drink and forget what has been ordained

> And infringe on the rights of the poor. . . .
> Open your mouth, judge righteously,
> And champion the poor and needy. (Proverbs 31:1–9)

The identity of the queen mother and king is much debated, but the provenance of this passage is impossible to determine with certainty. Taking the translation of Lemuel's name to mean "towards (*lemo*) God, (*'el*)" one who is dedicated to him, the midrashic commentators identify these royal personages as Solomon and Bathsheba. The rabbis project onto the figure of Bathsheba a maternal influence and assume that she encouraged her son, Solomon, to observe God's teachings. She is presumed to have warned him against women and wine, and to have instructed him to help the needy and to dispense justice to the oppressed.[23] Taking his mother's advice to heart, Solomon would be a man "going toward God" and thus become worthy of the name "Lemuel." These verses illustrate the queen mother's wisdom and the midrash further develops her influence.

Another biblical book attributed by tradition to King Solomon is the Song of Songs. In a scene depicting the joyful festivities of his wedding, the mother's participation in the ceremony is unexpectedly central. Since it was the royal prerogative of the king to crown his son one would expect the father to place the crown on his son's head. This is not the case however. It is Solomon's mother, Bathsheba who is accorded the honor of crowning her son:

> Go forth, O ye daughters of Zion
> And look upon King Solomon
> And upon the crown his mother set upon his head
> On the day of his wedding,
> The day of the gladness of his heart.
>
> (Song of Songs 3:11)

The coronation scene suggests a unique break in protocol. As described earlier, based on the first chapter of 1 Kings, it is clear that Solomon's mother Bathsheba was instrumental in assuring his accession to the throne. Although from the written account in the book of 1 Kings 1: 32–40 we do not know whether she participated in the actual coronation ceremony; it could be that the wedding scene here depicted in Song of Songs is connected closely with the coronation.

Another poetic description of a king's coronation that adds to our understanding of mother-queen and son relationships is found in Psalm 45. Scholars conjecture as to the identity of the king and his royal "consort" (*shegel*). Though it is impossible to determine with any certainty, some commentators posit that the king in question is Solomon and the consort the daughter of an Egyptian pharaoh. Others suggest that the king and consort referred to are Ahab and Jezebel.[24] Our point in mentioning Psalm 45 is simply to acknowledge that other biblical descriptions attach nuptial contracts to royal coronation, and to note the important role the queen mother may have played in both ceremonies (based on the evidence of Song of Songs 3).

The scenes in the historical books of Kings and even the more speculative interpretations that identify some biblical texts in Proverbs and Song of Songs with Solomon and Bathsheba suggest a very close relationship between mother and son. Might this relationship reveal a typical connection between other kings and their queen mothers who play an active and influential role at court? Indeed, some commentators take the figure of Solomon in Song of Songs as an archetype and his relationship with Bathsheba as typical of that between a king and his mother.[25]

The Bible features other examples of royal mothers who enjoy power at court. Two generations after Bathsheba, we read of Maacah, the mother of Abijah, king of Judah. Unlike the harmonious relationship between Bathsheba and Solomon, the relationship between this queen mother and her son is fraught with conflict. One cause of their underlying disagreement stems from Maacah's involvement in idol worship. The Asherah cult that Maacah promotes at the Judean court centers around a stylized tree in the form of the goddess. The queen mother's cultic practices angers King Asa, who is either her son or grandson. While it is difficult to determine the exact genealogy of Maacah in relation to Asa, it is clear that his being king has the power to depose her from her position as queen mother (1 Kings 15:2,10, 13; 2 Chr. 11:20; 15:16).[26] Asa deposes her as Maacah failed to carry out her duties in accordance with the laws of Judah, which opposes worship of the Asherah cult.[27] The biblical account demonstrates that after the king deposes her, Maacah loses the rights to the honorific title of *gevirah* by which she had formerly been addressed. Her removal from the honored rank of *gevirah* serves as the basis for Ackerman's theory that the queen mother does indeed occupy an actual court position. While it remains evident that Maacah as queen mother has power at the royal court, she iscertainly less influential than the king who has the ultimate authority. From the example of Maacah we see just how secure the queen mother's status is. Her position is firmly established so long as she acts in accordance with religious practices sanctioned by the biblical narrators and as long as she did not antagonize the king.

Two other powerful queen mothers appear in the days of Jeremiah when Babylon threatened Judah: Hamutal and Nehushta. Hamutal was the wife of the pious King Josiah and mother of two wicked sons, Jehoahaz and Zedekiah (2 Kings: 23:31; 24:18; Jer. 52:1). The prophet Jeremiah decries the wickedness of her sons and especially of Zedekiah, who, according to Jeremiah, "did what was displeasing in the eyes of God" (Jer. 52:1–2). Their specific iniquities are never detailed. Nevertheless, the first son Jehoahaz is deposed and taken in chains to Riblah by Pharaoh Necho, King of Egypt. Nebuchadnezzar, the Babylonian king, has Zedekiah's sons put to death right before his very eyes and then has Zedekiah's eyes put out before being carried off to Babylon. Hamutal's influence as queen mother is not described, nor is her relationship with her ill-fated sons articulated. National events overshadow the particulars of their individual lives in the last dark days leading up to the destruction of Judah in the sixth century BCE.

During the difficult era before Judah's devastation, Nehushta, the daughter of El-Nathan of Jerusalem and mother of King Jehoiakin, is the last queen mother to hold the title *gevirah* (2 Kings 24:8). The prophet Jeremiah foretells the fate of the king and the queen mother, as he proclaims: "Say to the king and the *gevirah* 'Take a lowly seat, for your beautiful '*atarah* (crown) has come down from your head' " (Jer, 13:18). This phrase as well as Jeremiah 29:2 are usually cited to argue the high status and centrality of the queen mother, in both places referred to as *gevirah*. The verse implies that the *gevirah* was wearing a crown like the king, and that the enemy regarded her as equally powerful and dangerous, to the point of exiling her to Babylon together with the king, the court and important subjects (2 Kings 24:12). Though King Jehoiakin is deposed and deported, the Babylonian monarch Evil-morodoch, son of Nebuchadnezzar, eventually restores Jehoiakin to a place of honor within the society of the captive kings being held in the Babylonian court (2 Kings 25:27–30). The partial restoration of her son's honor may have brightened Nehushta's years of captivity.

Before leaving the subject of queen mothers we should mention two powerful women, Jezebel and Athalya, who are both close to a king though do not fit squarely into the queen mother archetype. The former is the infamous wife of King Ahab, and the latter is their daughter, the only woman to rule Judah.

Jezebel, queen to King Ahab of Israel, introduced her Phoenician cult and culture into the Northern Kingdom in the mid-ninth century BCE. Her cultic activities brought her into sharp conflict with the Prophet Elijah, who instructed his disciple Elisha to bring down the House of Ahab in order to eliminate the cult of Baal. Jezebel's syncretistic practices made her name a synonym for wickedness (1 Kings 16–21; 2 Kings 9). Although I have posited that the institution of queen mother did not exist in the Northern Kingdom, messengers from Judah call her *gevirah*. Perhaps they imported this honorific from the southern tradition to which they were accustomed.

Athalya, daughter of Ahab and Jezebel, granddaughter of Omri and mother of King Ahaziah, is actually the only woman who ruled as queen in Judah

(2 Kings 11:3). This point must be emphasized. Her son Ahaziah is wounded and dies at the hand of Jehu, who had been designated by Elisha to destroy the house of Ahab for its sins. When she sees her son die, she seizes the throne of Judah and resolves to destroy "all royal seed" (2 Kings11:1). She knew that if one of her sons or grandsons, the young princes, became king, her place as queen mother would be usurped. She succeeds in destroying the royal seed and crowns herself ruler of the land. Though her name means "God is exalted," as queen ruler she promotes the worship of Baal in Judah as her mother had done in the Northern Kingdom of Israel (2 Kings 11:1–20: 2 Chron.22:2–12; 23:12–21; 24:7). Athalya manages to sit on the throne for six years and is eventually deposed by the priests.

Athalya plants a seed of evil in the kingdom that influences rulers of future generations who will continue to resurrect the cult of Baal, but she is unable to corrupt the ruling house altogether. The high priest's wife Jehosheba hides the one child who escapes the carnage wrought by Athalya. He eventually becomes Joash, King of Judah. The legacy of the sole female ruler is sadly recorded in 2 Chronicles 24:7, "For the children of the wicked Athalya had violated the House of God and had even used the sacred objects for the worship of Baal" (2 Chron. 24:7). The sources in Kings and Chronicles denigrate Athalya, yet her absolute rule for several years was a circumstance unprecedented in all the history of Israel and Judah until the time of the Hasmoneans. Although her influence was negative, we must at least acknowledge that she achieved a great measure of power unseen before her time. As a woman, she attained much power and the impact of her rule was felt for years later.

CONCLUSION

Presented here is a galaxy of wise and valorous women acting as queen mothers and as household and community leaders. We first looked at the book of Proverbs, traditionally attributed to Solomon, which contains descriptions and portrays scenes that remind one of Bathsheba, the queen mother. The book opens as it does with many personifications of wise women and closes with the picture of the ideal woman who is a trusted wife, devoted mother and sagacious counselor.

We started out our discussion looking at examples of wise women. These women wield influence in both the private sector and the public realm. The narratives involving the wise women of Tekoa and Abel, depicted mothers in biblical Israel who ventured out beyond their domestic gates into the public square and into the royal court as widely-respected defenders and advisors to king and commoner. The stories of the two mothers who came to King

Solomon and Rizpa, are Wisdom stories dealing with the challenges of motherhood under difficult conditions. The accounts involving other lesser known queen mothers (Maacah, Hamutal, Nehushta) also shed light on the topic in that we see how they influenced court life. We finally look at a few examples of somewhat destructive female figures associated with royal life. These women greatly influenced society, albeit negatively.

After our discussion on wise women, we analyzed the lives of the queen mothers. We next saw that the power of the king's mother was acknowledged not only by her royal son in a familial context, but also by the larger public in the realm of politics and religion. Whether she had an official position or not is still being debated by scholars, but her role as counselor is beyond question. These mothers are mental and emotional pillars of strength behind their sons. Often the son's rule reflects well on the mother, and thus, the queen mother enjoys power and influence at court.

The vast majority of narratives we analyzed illustrate how, in biblical times, mothers, acting in the capacity of wise woman or queen mother, responded in a positive and powerful manner to urgent needs of society and made their influence felt in social, religious, and political spheres.

NOTES

1. Though both the figures of wisdom and folly are personified in Proverbs as women, we isolate the woman of wisdom and leave the woman of folly for a later study.

2. Wisdom, as a literary image, is feminine in other Ancient Near Eastern cultures as well. It is usually associated with goddesses or assigned titles such as Lady Knowledge who is thought to be pursued like a human woman might be pursued. See *Encyclopedia of Women and World Religion*, Vol. 2, ed. Serinity Young (New York, New York: Macmillan Reference USA, 1999), 1031, s.v. Wisdom.

3. Claudia Camp, "Wisdom and the Feminine in the Book of Proverbs," *Bible and Literature Series,* no.11 (Sheffield, England: Almond Press, 1985), 288, 290.

4. A. Brenner, "Some Observations on the Figurations of woman in Wisdom Literature," in *Of Prophets' Visions and the Wisdom of Sages: Essays in Honour of R. Norman Whybray on His Seventieth Birthday*, ed. by Heather McKay and David Clines (Sheffield: JSOT Press, 1993), 192–208

5. See also Proverbs 10:1; 15:20; 19:26; 20:20; 23:22, 25. In all these passages, the mother's claim to respect is equal to the father's.

6. Many translations use "mother-city," but we prefer here Young's translation: "a city and a mother" (*Young's Analytical Concordance to the Bible*, [Eerdman's Publishing, 1978]), 169.

7. Susan Ackerman, *Warrior, Dancer, Seductress, Queen* (New York: Doubleday, 1998), 40. See also p. 78, note 42, *Genesis Rab.* 94,9, and de Boer, "The Counsellor," op.cit., 60.

8. 2 Kings 18:18; Isaiah 36:1 – 22; see also 2 Samuel 11:18–28.

9. Phyllis Trible, *God and the Rhetoric of Sexuality* (Philadelphia, Pennsylvania: Fortress Press, 1978), 33.

10. The Bible tells of fathers coming face to face with death of sons. For example, Aaron witnesses the death of Nadav and Abihu (Leviticus 10:3), David's child from Batsheva dies (2 Samuel 12:18), and David also loses Abshalom (2 Sam. 19:1), whom he laments: "O, Absalom,! If only I had died instead of you!"

11. Although the bible records that Michal, daughter of Saul has no children (2 Samuel 6:22), commentators reconciled this verse by claiming either that she is a gloss for her sister or Merab or that she brought up Merab's five sons, and therefore merited the title "mother."

12. *The Anchor Bible Dictionary*, vol. 5 (New York: Doubleday, 1992), 583–586, s.v. "Queen."

13. Athalya Brenner mentions other queen mothers of the ancient near east, the mothers of the Assyrian kings Semiramis and Nitokris; *The Israelite Woman* (Sheffield: JSOT Press, 1985), 20.

14. Niels-Erik Andreasen, "The Role of the Queen Mother in Israelite Society," *Catholic Biblical Quarterly*, vol. 45, no. 2, (April 1983), 179–194.

15. Leonard H. Lesko, "The Egyptian New Kingdom," in *Women's Earliest Records from Ancient Egypt and Western Asia* (Atlanta: Scholar's Press, 1989), 101. Lesko points out that the Egyptian Eighteenth Dynasty was "formidably feminine," being ruled by various female personalities, notably, Pharaoh Hatshepsut, but Queen Tiy, consort of Amenhotep III, and their daughter-in-law Nefertiti, who acted as chief royal wives are also worthy of mentioning here.

16. Zafrira Ben-Barak, "The Status and Right of the Gebira," in *A Feminist Companion to Samuel and Kings*, ed. Athalya Brenner (Sheffield, England: Sheffield Academic Press, 1994), 170ff.

17. Niels-Erik A. Andreasen, *Ibid.*, 187.

18. Manuals of instruction for kings and princes are well known from ancient Near East, but nowhere is it addressed to a king by his mother. See James Pritchard, *Ancient Near Eastern Texts* (Princeton, New Jersey: Princeton University Press, 1955), 414–418.

19. Susan Ackerman, "The Queen Mother and the Cult in Ancient Israel," in *Women in the Hebrew Bible*, ed. Alice Bach (New York and London, England: Rutledge, 1999), 179.

20. See list of the names of the Queen mothers in *The Anchor Bible Dictionary*, vol. 5, *ibid.*, 585, s.v. Queen.

21. *The Anchor Bible Dictionary*, vol. 4, *ibid.*, 71.

22. A similar incident of a rift over a king's concubine is narrated between King Saul's Commander-in-Chief Abner and Saul's son Ishboshet which will be discussed later in the same chapter (2 Samuel 3:7–9; 2 Samuel 21: 4–14). See also Abshalom who possessed his father David's concubines on the advice of Ahithophel to symbolize that he would be king.

23. See Ibn Ezra. *Mikraot Gedolot: Mishle* 30–1 (New York: Pardes Publishing House, 1951), 134; *Numbers Rab.*, (London, England: Soncino, 1983), Chap. 10:3–4; *Ecclesiates Rab.* Chap. 1:1, para. 2.

24. Derek Kidner, *Psalms 1–72: An Introduction and Commentary on Books I and II of the Psalms* (Leicester: Intervarsity Press, 1976), 170–174. For more possible candidates regarding the identity of bride and groom in Psalm 45, please see Arthur Weiser, *The Psalms* (London: SCM Press, 1949), 362.

25. Michael V. Fox, *The Song of Songs and the Ancient Egyptian Love Songs* (Madison, Wisconsin: University of Wisconsin Press, 1985), 120–132.

26. *The Anchor Bible*, op. cit., 429, s.v. Maacah

27. This incursion of the Ashera cult appears to have remained a problem for subsequent reformer kings like Hezekiah in the eighth century BCE and Josiah in the seventh century BCE although the records do not claim that their mothers were involved in this cult.

Chapter Four

Mothers and Daughters

Like mother like daughter.

Ezekiel 16:44

To bear, to nurse, to rear, to watch and then to lose, to see my bright ones disappear drawn up like morning dews.

J.INGELOW, *Songs of Seven: Seven Times Six*

What does the Hebrew Bible tell us about mothers and daughters? This question is surprisingly difficult to answer. Although we find many interactions between fathers and sons, mothers and sons, and even fathers and daughters in the Bible, it records only a few interactions between mothers and daughters. Biblical narrators often portray women yearning to bear sons but do not depict parents as wanting daughters. In reading through the Bible, we might infer that daughters are not as important as sons to the continuation of the nation, and therefore, they are less desired than boys.[1] Is this impression further substantiated by the scant traces of mother and daughter relationships in the Bible? By bringing into focus the few instances of mother-daughter interactions, I hope to explore what roles a biblical mother plays in relation to a daughter, and in accumulating this information, show that some daughters were indeed both longed for, and a consequential part of the family unit.

We begin by mentioning the mother-daughter metaphor used for the relationship between God and Israel that occurs throughout the Bible. We then discuss the mother in the general statements about parent-child relationships in the Bible. From there, we consider three daughters whose mothers are named in the Bible: Miriam, daughter of Jochebed, Dinah, daughter of Leah; and Tamar, daughter of Maacah.[2] Finally, we look at Ruth and the Song of

Songs, two books in the Bible that along with the story of Rebecca as daughter quite unexpectedly provide examples of positive mother-daughter relationships.

GOD AS MOTHER, ISRAEL AS DAUGHTER: A METAPHORICAL RELATIONSHIP

There is both a metaphorical dimension and actual dimension to the topic of mothers and daughters. In fact, the Bible makes more use of the metaphorical daughter, than of the actual daughter. We want to deal with the metaphoric dimension of the topic because it may shed some light on how mother-daughter relationships should be viewed within biblical literature.

On the occasions when the word *bat* (daughter) appears in the Bible, it may refer either to an actual person or to an abstraction (e.g., a nation, a poetic persona).[3] *Bat* is often used in poetic epithets that personify cities and nations—the most commonly occurring combinations are *bat siyyon* (daughter of Zion), *bat yerushalayim* (daughter of Jerusalem), and *bat 'ammi* (daughter of my people).[4] The personification of the people as a daughter has something to do with the structure of the Hebrew language. The gender of the words for countries and cities is feminine, and the prophets capitalized on that grammatical fact in their poetry. What does the personified daughter of the prophets do? She cries and rejoices, sneers and minces. She is always embedded in emotions and is shown only in the roles that express the (collective) emotional life of the nation of Israel.[5] In other words, the metaphorical daughter is a public rather than a private figure.[6] The negative side of this portrayal is that when the nation of Zion falls away from God, the daughter of Zion appears as a fallen woman.

The figure of the daughter of Zion and the metaphorical association of God with the figure of the mother are connected at only one point: they are both shown as a woman giving birth. The literary prophets make much use of this birthing metaphor. The *bat- siyyon*, though often liked to a virgin, also is seen as a woman in pain and travail, laboring to give birth. "Zion travailed, and at once she bore her children! Shall I who bring on labor not bring about birth, says the Lord?" (Isaiah 66:7–9) God, playing a motherly role, is also depicted as giving birth. Exilic Isaiah (chapters 40–66) resonates with imagery of God travailing in labor and, in a maternal way, comforting the people. In Isaiah 42:13 God says, "Now I will scream like a woman in labor, I will pant and I will gasp."[7]

The metaphorical imagery used in the Bible to refer to Israel as daughter is instructive for us. As a daughter, Israel is obliged to submit, obey, and live within strict perimeters of biblical law. The daughter, then, (both the metaphorical one and the actual one) never has power. This is why this image of daughter, rather than the image of son, was chosen as a metaphor to represent Israel.

Whenever a feminine role is attributed to God, it is always *mother*[8] but never *wife*.[9] Moreover, the Bible seems to strictly divide the mothering role for God from any erotic role. God the mother never has any marital dimension, just as Zion the daughter never has any private dimension. Instead, the Bible seems comfortable with portraying God as both mother and father, perhaps to suggest that each role was equally authoritative. As we have been discussing, the mother of ancient Israel has both domestic and national power, and when the biblical narrators choose to depict God as a mother figure, they demonstrate knowledge of maternal authority.

Despite the common association of the image of the mother with God and the image of the daughter with the nation of Israel and Zion, we cannot find any place where God the mother is mothering Zion the daughter. This is, in fact, in keeping with most of the Bible. The Bible does, however, attach some significance to the actual (rather than metaphorical) mother-daughter relationship, as we will see below. Although mother-son relationships dominate the biblical landscape and demonstrate the power mothers gain, mother-daughter relationships show a different aspect of the biblical mother. Examining the mother-daughter relationship portrayed in the Bible shows us yet another dimension of the mother's behavior and influence within the family.

A DAUGHTER IN THE HOUSEHOLD

Statements about parenting in the Bible generally concern the discipline and the marriage of children. The mother is included in several of the mandates to children about honoring parents, beginning with the commandment "Honor thy father and thy mother."[10] Only two passages mention the mother vis-à-vis her daughter explicitly. One says that the mother of a daughter shall be regarded as unclean for twice as long as the mother of a son (Lev. 12:2–5). The other states that "the girl's father and mother shall produce the evidence of the girl's virginity" (Deut. 22:13) if a man declares that the girl was not a virgin when he married her. The mother drops out of sight immediately in this case, however, possibly because the biblical narrators recognize the father, but not the mother, as a public figure.[11] Only the father goes before the elders to provide the proof of the daughter's virginity, and if the daughter is found guilty she is severely punished (Deut. 22:17, 21). The daughter's fate is placed in the hands of her father, and her mother is mostly absent from the narrative, with occasional exception as mentioned below.

Such mandates are intermittently supplemented by more informal instructions to parents and children. For example, in Micah 7:6, the complete despair of the prophet is communicated through his vision of the disintegration of the family:

> For son spurns father,
> Daughter rises up against mother,
> Daughter-in-law against mother-in-law—
> A man's own household
> Are his enemies.

Note how the daughter is paired with the mother, the son with the father—even in rebellion the Bible divides the sexes. Similarly, the proverb "Like mother, like daughter" (Ezek. 16:44–45) segregates the sexes in order to visit the sins of the mother on her daughter. Proverbs gives importance to the mother's instructions, but does not mention how these instructions impact a daughter. The text admonishes only the son to "not forsake your mother's teaching"—the daughter goes unmentioned. Daughters in the Bible are not depicted as recipients of instruction outside of the home.

In the general discussions of the parent-child relationship in the Bible, we catch glimpses of the mother-daughter relationship, but more often, note its absence. While the text implies that the daughter is under the supervision of the mother, the most pivotal decisions in a daughter's life are made by the father; for instance, he decides whom she will marry, and other major life issues. We are given very little sense of the day-to-day interaction of mothers and daughters or of the responsibilities of the mother toward the daughter. For the most part, we are left to our imagination.[12]

VISIBLE MOTHERS AND DAUGHTERS: THREE STORIES

Only three biblical stories feature a daughter whose mother's name is recorded: Miriam, Dinah, and Tamar. In contrast, Achsah, Jephthah's daughter, the Levite's concubine, and so many of the other daughters in the Bible do not have named mothers. Given that naming implies importance in the Bible, the stories of Dinah, Miriam, and Tamar give us the rare opportunity to explore the biblical mother-daughter relationship.

The first mother and daughter—Jochebed and Miriam—remain unnamed in the narrative for a long time, but this is true for all the participants in the story of Exodus 2: Moses is named first (Ex. 2:10, by the daughter of Pharaoh), then his brother Aaron (Ex. 4:14), then his parents Amram and Jochebed together (Ex. 6:20). Pharaoh's daughter is never named,[13] and

Miriam is not named until very late. She is even left out of the genealogy in Ex. 6:20 after the parting of the Red Sea: "Miriam the prophetess, Aaron's sister" (Ex. 15:20). In fact, we are only able to infer retrospectively from Numbers 26:58 that Miriam is the sister in Exodus 2 who waits to see Moses' fate and brings their mother to Pharaoh's daughter as a wet nurse. This is as close as the narrative gets to an interaction between this daughter and her mother, and although we assume that the daughter is acting in sympathy with her mother, even this is speculation. Jochebed and Amram both disappear from the narrative immediately, and neither is shown interacting with their children.[14] All three children go on to have brilliant careers. Although God speaks mostly to Moses and Aaron, Miriam is accorded the significant role of prophetess and leader. Neither parent—mother or father—plays a dominant role in the lives of any their children.

The portrait of Miriam shows a woman who is inventive and shrewd. As scholars have noted,[15] the women in Exodus are all resourceful, wise, and defiant in the face of the oppression of the Egyptian overlords.[16] Miriam is certainly no exception. Jochebed's daughter, Miriam, had the dubious advantage of growing up at a time when the birth of a son was a painful and futile event, for Pharaoh had decreed, "'Every boy that is born you shall throw into the Nile, but let every girl live'" (Ex. 1:22). She experiences the oppression of the Israelites under Egyptian rule, and even witnesses the suffering her mother must have endured as she laid her baby boy in a basket and watched the basket float on the banks of the river. As she watches the action from a distance, Miriam thinks up a plan by which her mother can take part in the upbringing of Moses, offering to find a Hebrew wet nurse for Pharaoh's daughter. We can only imagine the emotional interactions that certainly took place between mother and daughter. It is a situation fraught with gender politics and poignant possibilities that the narrative, unfortunately, does not explore. Did Miriam follow her baby brother's basket at her mother's bidding? Did she come up with the plan on her own, because of her devotion to the baby? We may speculate, but the text remains silent.

This failure on the part of the biblical narrator to follow up on extraordinary narrative possibilities occurs again in the stories of Dinah and Tamar. Both of these stories involve an extraordinary event—a scandal or a tragedy—that apparently motivated their inclusion in the biblical record. In the stories of Dinah and Tamar, the themes of rape and incest are played out—with visible consequences in the public as well as the private sphere. Dinah is the daughter of Jacob, the patriarchal head over the twelve tribes, and Leah, his unloved first wife. She is the last of Leah's children, the only girl, and the only one of Leah's children whose name is not given an etiology in the Bible (Gen. 30:21)—all of which augurs an unfortunate future for this child. The next incident of Dinah's life recorded in the Bible is her rape by Shechem, the son of a chief of the region (Gen. 4:1–31). Susan Niditch notes that Dinah is, "on the one hand, central to the action, the focus of Shechem's desire, the object of negotiations between Jacob and Hamor, the reason for her brothers' trickery, and the cause of tension between Jacob and his sons. On the other hand, she has no dialogue, no voice. . . . She seems to fade out after her brothers retrieve her."[17] This is a summary of the biblical narrative, which highlights the fact that Leah participates neither in protesting nor in avenging of Dinah's rape. Today, the story of the rape of a daughter might well include her mother's reaction, but this is not the case in the androcentric world of the Bible. This is one incident where the mother's voice is silent, absent, lacking. The mother participates only indirectly and in only one way: She has produced the sons, Simeon and Levi, who negotiate with their sister's rapist and make sure that he does not go unpunished. While the biblical narrative focuses on the action of each scene, the reader is anxious to know whether there was any scene of consolation between the father and daughter or the mother and daughter to assuage the anguish of violation. The text remains sadly silent. Leah's only action reported in the life of the daughter was to name her Dinah, from the Hebrew word din, "judgment," and indeed, a cruel judgment overcame her.

Dinah's father Jacob has the authority to speak, but the horror of the event overwhelms him, so that we read that Jacob, when told of the rape, "kept silent until [his sons] came home" (Gen. 34:5). A conversation between Jacob and his sons may have ensued, but the text does not record what they said. Instead, the narrator just says that "Jacob's sons answered Shechem and his father Hamor" (Gen. 34:13). It is Dinah's brothers who are quick to defend her reputation, while her father plays a passive role. Throughout, Jacob is depicted as acting expediently and diplomatically (Gen. 34:30), while Simon and Levi react vociferously and violently. They ask Jacob, "Should our sister be treated like a whore?" (Gen. 34:31), and they destroy the nation of the Hivites in retribution for their sister's dishonor. Simeon and Levi, the two brothers of Dinah by Leah, seem to take great offense at her rape. The siblings who share the same mother are deeply attached. Though the Bible does not make much of this connection, but there is much to be read between the lines. Of all of Jacob's sons, it is notably his two sons by Leah that act to aid her daughter and their sister.

Years later, on his deathbed, Jacob recalls this incident when talking to his sons (Gen. 49:5–7):

> Simeon and Levi are a pair;
> Their weapons are tools of lawlessness.

> Let not my person be included in their council,
> Let not my being be counted in their assembly.
> For when angry they slay men,
> And when pleased they maim oxen.
> Cursed be their anger so fierce,
> And their wrath so relentless.
> I will divide them in Jacob,
> Scatter them in Israel.

As a result of their violent actions, one of which was their response to the rape of their sister,[18] Simeon seems to be excluded from having specified tribal territories, and Levi is given the singular blessing of service in the temple instead of land. The consequences of Simeon and Levi's response to their sister's rape are far-reaching. But what happens to Dinah? Her name appears in the list of the descendants of Jacob who came into Egypt (Gen. 46:8, 15), but the Bible makes no further mention of her.[19] The biblical story plays out the meaning of her name, "judged" or "avenged"—others act on her behalf and make decisions about her—and then she disappears from the narrative.[20]

Later tradition discusses to what extent Dinah's parents were responsible for her rape, noting that Leah was a bit forward and suggesting that perhaps her daughter was too. But more important is the rabbis' strengthening of the father's responsibility. They argue that Jacob's delay in returning to his father, Isaac, is the cause of all the bad things that happen to Jacob, and the rape of his daughter is just one of the evils that befall him.[21] Needless to say, the commentators do not recognize that the greatest evil befell not Jacob, but Dinah!

As in the story of Dinah, in the story of Tamar, brothers rather than mothers take the prominent parts. The opening verses set the scene by naming the three most important characters in the story: Absalom, Tamar, and Amnon (2 Sam. 13). They share the same father, King David, and from information provided elsewhere, we know that Amnon's mother is Ahinoam (2 Sam. 3:2), while the mother of Tamar and Absalom is Maacah (2 Sam. 3:3). Seeing that Amnon's infatuation with his half-sister is making him ill, a cousin of all three siblings advises Amnon to feign illness so that, when King David comes to visit, Amnon can ask his father to send Tamar to him. King David sends Tamar to Amnon's quarters, where she bakes and serves him cakes. Having sent all his attendants away, he grabs her and says, "'Come lie with me, sister!'" She protests, struggles, and argues, but to no avail. She asks, "'Where will I carry my shame? And you, you will be like any of the scoundrels in Israel!'" (2 Sam. 13:13).

After raping her, Amnon's feelings for Tamar shift abruptly from lust to hate and disgust. He tells his attendants, "'Get this thing out of my presence, and bar the door behind her'" (2 Sam. 13:17). She walks away, screaming and tearing her clothes. Whereas Shechem's desire for Dinah had in it an element of love, the story of Tamar begins with Amnon's lust and ends with his loathing. According to one Mosaic law, a man was obligated to marry a woman he raped and could never divorce her (Deut. 22:28–29; cf. Ex. 22:16), and it also prohibits sexual relations between siblings with the same father. But the pivotal question in this story is why Amnon's lust suddenly turns to hatred, a question that is surpassed only by King David's puzzling lack of response. Why does Amnon's lust turn to loathing? The narrative in some respects seems to anticipate modern theory about rape as an act of violence rather than love or lust: Amnon hates Tamar for failing to prevent him from harming her, for reminding him of his own weakness and sinfulness.[22] The rabbis shared the view that Amnon's behavior was violent and loathsome. They were so appalled by his actions that they create motivation for his strong hatred. They empower Tamar to punish Amnon by physically maiming him in such a way as to impair his virility,[23] and they discuss at length what they consider to be Tamar's understandable desire for revenge.

Neither the biblical narrator nor the rabbis bring the mother directly into the narrative to comfort Tamar, as we might expect today. As we saw in the story of Dinah, the mother's words, if there were any, are not recorded. Tamar's brother Absalom is the first and only one to speak to her: "'Was it your brother Amnon who did this to you? For the present, sister, keep quiet about it; he is your brother. Don't brood over the matter'" (2 Sam.13:20). There is no direct communication and little warmth between King David and Tamar, especially by modern Western standards.[24] Why is it that King David visits Amnon when he claims to be sick but remains aloof from his daughter who's been raped? (2 Sam.13:6) We learn that King David is vexed by the violation but he does not comfort Tamar and, although as king he has the power to punish Amnon, he does not (2 Sam 13); his response communicates neither empathy for Tamar nor outrage at Amnon's immorality.[25] Absalom is the one who acts on Tamar's behalf—he advises her, he takes her under his protection, and when it becomes clear that King David intended no consequences, two years later he has his servants kill Amnon. That Absalom and Tamar have the same mother may at least partially account for the protection that Absalom extends to Tamar. Perhaps the siblings were intimately connected in their great love and devotion to their common mother. Thus, Absalom's fight for Tamar's honor may be intertwined with the defense of the honor of their mother and in this way, through the figure of the brother, the mother-daughter connection can be detected. Though Tamar expected the shame of her rape would affect Amnon as well as herself, in the end the king does nothing. Her mother is not present either, but perhaps she is the driving force behind Absalom's efforts.

Like Jacob in the midrash cited above, David is complicit in his daughter's fate. In both cases, the sins of the father are visited upon their children—their daughters are raped and their sons commit terrible sins—and the fathers bear all the consequences without intervening directly. Dinah and Tamar are pawns of a larger patriarchal complex. They suffer horribly, their brothers attempt to defend them, and their fathers all but ignore their tragic fates. It is hard for a modern Western audience to fathom a father who would act so indifferently in light of the suffering of his beloved daughter. Our study of these two incidents thus sheds light on the particular relationship (or lack thereof) between the daughters and the mothers.

What is interesting in the stories of Dinah and Tamar is that the psychological and emotional components wrapped up in the action are displaced from the daughters onto her brothers by virtue of their relationship to one mother. The brothers are authoritative agents who often speak on behalf of their female relatives, as in the case of Rebecca whose brother (here along with her mother) aids in making the decision whether she should leave her father's house (Gen.24:55–59). In the stories of Dinah and Tamar, the brothers play dominant roles in which they express outrage at the mistreatment of their beloved sister, often carrying out judgment that she would be unable to execute on her own. In neither case is it clear that the brothers act in accordance with their sister's (or mother's) wishes, but it is possible that the brothers act as protectors for their maternal sister in accordance with their mother's wishes.[26]

RUTH AND THE SONG OF SONGS: A PARADIGM OF MOTHER AND DAUGHTER LOVE

Above we dealt with biblical women whose mothers are known and named. Now we turn our attention to women in the books of Ruth and Song of Songs, who offer us a beautiful picture of mother-daughter relationships. The following discussion elaborates on the relations between women when the sons and the fathers incidentally died. Although some scholars do not detect a biological mother-daughter relationship between Naomi and Ruth, others accept that Naomi's status as mother-in-law creates a strong familial bond between the two women equal in emotional and social scope to a biological affiliation.

The scroll of Ruth presents us with a case of a daughter-in-law who finds herself without a male protector in the form of a father-in-law or husband, as both figures had died. As Ruth's story unfolds, we see that she is indeed a unique woman. She is the epitome of *hesed*, "loving-kindness," and she is the only female foreigner to have a biblical book named for her. After Ruth's husband tragically dies, the first impulse of her mother-in-law, Naomi, is to send her daughters-in-law away. Naomi says to them, " 'Turn back, each of you to her mother's house. May the Lord deal kindly with you, as you have dealt with the dead and with me! May the Lord grant that each of you find security in the house of a husband!' And she kissed them farewell. They broke into weeping" (Ruth 1:8–9). Again we have women in the midst of tragedy, but the contrast is startling. Tamar and Dinah are surrounded by men who are violent. Of the few kind words spoken in their stories, none are spoken by women. At the beginning of the book of Ruth, we suddenly see words of kindness spoken between the female characters.

Ruth is a unique story in the Bible of two women choosing to be together as mother and daughter even after their formal familial ties have been sundered. Although in the beginning of the story, Ruth cleaves stubbornly to Naomi, Naomi eventually grows attached to Ruth. Naomi calls Ruth "daughter" and is concerned about Ruth's future. She tells Ruth, "'Daughter, I must seek a home for you, where you may be happy'" (Ruth 3:1). Although Ruth refers to Naomi neither as "mother" nor as "mother-in-law," she allows Naomi to function as her mother throughout the narrative, and her devotion to Naomi is evident and unconditional from the start of the book:[27]

> Do not entreat me to leave you, to turn back from following you. For where you go, I will go; wherever you lodge, I will lodge; your people shall be my people and your God my God; where you die I will die and there I will be buried. Thus and more may God do to me if anything but death parts you and me (Ruth 1:16–18).

The loyalty between these women is extraordinary by any standards, but it is particularly notable given that the Bible rarely records scenes of loyalty or kindness between women.[28] What are we to make of the fact that the narrators of the book of Ruth explicitly have these two women play the roles of mother and daughter? Is it that the Bible can only imagine female friendship, especially between women of different generations, in terms of mothers and daughters? Or does the Bible hold up the mother-daughter relationship as a paradigm of love, namely, that at their best, humans will care for one another *as if* they were mother and daughter? Before we can begin to answer such questions, however, we have to address another problem: that it is hard to know exactly what comprises "daughterly" and "motherly" behavior in the Bible because we see so few mother-daughter relationships depicted. The dialogue between Ruth and Naomi is about mundane matters, and yet to modern ears it seems full of love. The mother says: tell me about your day, do this so you will be safer, do that so you can be married (Ruth 2:19–23; 3:1ff). The daughter says: I went to work, I met this man, this is what he said to me, this is what he did.[29]

Throughout the book, the women work toward material and emotional security. Ruth gleans in the fields to provide food for herself and Naomi, while Naomi advises Ruth how to obtain a worthy husband. Eventually, Naomi instructs Ruth thus: "'Wash therefore and anoint yourself, and put on your best clothes, and go down to the threshing floor'" (Ruth 3:3). Ruth responds, "'I will do everything you tell me'" (Ruth 3:5). Here we see a mother-daughter relationship presented positively and in great detail: each woman trusts in the judgment of the other, each willingly gambles for long-term material security for both of them and for the chance of a son who would continue the lineage. They together cooperate to exist as best they can in an androcentric system.

Indeed some scholars argue that the entire purpose of the Scroll of Ruth *is* the end: the birth of the son. The lineage established is full of strange quirks, however, including two foreign women. The scroll details the actions of one of these foreign women and has the elders explicitly remind Boaz and us of the actions of the other: "'And may your house be like the house of Perez whom Tamar bore to Judah'" (Ruth 4:12). Both Tamar and Ruth were childless widows. Tamar plays the harlot and Ruth similarly visits Boaz alone at night in order to call the male relative (redeemer) to account in helping her to conceive the necessary son. Boaz marries a foreign woman (a Moabite), who bears the son Obed who is named as the rightful heir and progenitor of the line of David by a chorus of women:

> Blessed be the LORD, who has not withheld a redeemer from you today! May his name be perpetuated in Israel! He will renew your life and sustain your old age; for he is born of your daughter-in-law, who loves you and is better to you than seven sons (Ruth 4:14–15).

The love of Ruth and Naomi provides the lineage of King David. It is they, not the men of the story, who shape the hope of the nation of Israel out of the hopelessness of their own situation. They draw sweetness out of bitterness and the agent of this transformation is love rather than jealousy, inclusion rather than exclusion.

A long and honored tradition views the story of Ruth and Naomi as a book about women working to re-establish the line of their dead husbands through redeemer responsibility and levirate marriage (when a widow of a man who died childless marries the man's brother or close relative to carry on her dead husband's lineage).[30] This is an important sociological element of the narrative throughout the scroll, and indeed the final four verses of the scroll introduce a genealogy that does not mention the women. The narrative of the scroll of Ruth may provide insight into the situation of foreign women and childless women among the Israelites. The story highlights women's economic pragmatism in the family.

Embedded in the Scroll of Ruth is the story of a particular cross-generational relationship between two women which includes the strongest articulation of love by a daughter for her mother and of a mother for her daughter: "He is born of your daughter-in-law, who loves you and means more to you than seven sons"(Ruth 4:15).[31] This very direct observation on the love between Ruth and Naomi harks back to their initial condition—before Naomi's sons died, before Ruth married Boaz, for Ruth's second marriage does not officially make Naomi either her mother or her mother-in-law but rather a relative by marriage. The articulation of Naomi's love for Ruth suggests that their initial relationship has become fixed, as if it they were biological relatives.

The *hesed* ("loving kindness") that characterizes the relationship between Ruth and Naomi spills over into other relationships described in the book. Boaz does not simply fulfill the legal requirements of levirate marriage—he acts out of kindness beyond duty. He was not the redeemer in line, but yet he chooses to redeem Ruth (4:1–5). The willingness of both members of this couple to accept obligations not incumbent upon them by law or custom makes them paragons of righteousness, living embodiments of *hesed*. If there were more mother-daughter relationships in the Bible, we could test a theory that the absence of the mother augurs danger for a daughter left to the mercy of men may wish to do her evil (e.g., Tamar and Dinah, see above; Jephthah's daughter in Judges 12:34–40; the Levite's concubine in Judges 19:1–20:6). The presence of the mother assures a daughter protection (e.g., Naomi and Ruth, Bethuel's wife and Rebecca). The only other place in the Bible to demonstrate that a daughter finds safety in her mother is in the Song of Songs.

The Songs of Songs comprises a number of love poems that dramatize an emotionally rather than narratively coherent story of the love between a young woman and her lover. The lovers perform a duet in which the woman usually leads, her lover answers, and various anonymous voices join in from time to time. Some of these poems generalize about love, while others praise the physical beauty of the lovers, speak of the difficulties and the ecstasies of their love, or envision the marriage rites of King Solomon. Over the ages, this book has been approached most often either as an allegory of the love of God for his people (partly in order to justify the inclusion of non-religious love poetry in the biblical canon) or as a sequence of erotic poetry celebrating the love of a man and a woman.

I want to focus, however, on the surprising importance in the Song of Songs of the woman's relationship to her mother and her brothers, and on how their relations correspond to as well as differ from patterns set up elsewhere in biblical literature. Ariel and Chana Bloch, in their translation of the scroll, lay out the daughter's place in the family:

> The Shulamite is her mother's favorite (6:9); when she speaks of her brothers, she calls them, in the Hebrew, "my mother's sons" (1:6); she wishes her lover were as close to her as a brother "who nursed at [her] mother's breast" (8:1). She brings her lover home to her "mother's house," perhaps to signify a more binding relationship (3:4, 8:2). She declares that she awakened her lover in the very place where his mother conceived and gave birth to him (8:5). Even King Solomon's mother appears in the poem, crowning her son on his wedding day (3:11). . . . The brothers [1:6, 2:15, 8:8–10] and the watchmen [3:3, 5:7] provide whatever friction there is in the poem. From the beginning, the Shulamite's brothers are watching her; as one would expect in a biblical text, they are their sister's keepers.[32]

The same configuration of characters as in the story of Naomi, Ruth, and Boaz—a mother, her daughter, the daughter's lover, and no father for the daughter—exists here with the notable addition of the daughter's brothers. A variation on the configurations of characters found in the stories of Rebecca, Tamar, and Dinah also exists here: Tamar and Dinah's stories never mention their mothers and center on the relations among the lover/rapist, father, and full brothers; Rebecca's story mentions her father Bethuel once but centers on the negotiations of her future husband's representatives with her full brother Laban and her (unnamed) mother. Every story has a different configuration of the family, and every story has the family act and react differently to the relationship between the daughter and her suitor. The stories of Dinah and Tamar are the tragic ones, and this is in part, as I have argued, because the mothers are missing from their stories.[33] For both, there is no voice of lovingkindness; for both, there is no refuge in the mother's house.

The word "mother's house" appears twice in the Song of Songs. In both cases, the daughter is talking to her lover: "I held him fast, I would not let him go / Till I brought him to my mother's house, / To the chamber of her who conceived me" (3:4); I would lead you, I would bring you / To the house of my mother, / Of her who taught me" (8:2).[34] The daughter may simply be eager to designate him as her official lover by introducing him to her mother,[35] but the language surrounding the term also indicates, that the daughter regards her mother's house as a place where love can and does reside and she believes she honors their love by bringing him home. Clearly, she expects acceptance from her mother, even if her mother's sons are not so accommodating ("My brothers were angry with me, / they made me guard the vineyards. / I have not guarded my own" [1:6]; "What shall we do for our sister / when suitors besiege her? / If she is a wall, we will build / a silver turret upon her. / If she is a door, we will bolt her / with beams of cedarwood" [8:8–9]; Bloch and Bloch trans.).

The term "mother's house" appears in only two other places in the Bible—in the stories of Ruth and Rebecca—where it is again linked to love, wisdom, women's agency, and marriage.[36] As we saw above, Naomi tells Orpah and Ruth, "Turn back, each of you to her mother's house'" (Ruth 1:8). It is not clear what associations Naomi has with the mother's house. Does she think of it as a place that will only reluctantly take in these bereft daughters-in-law? Or does she view it as a place where they will be warmly welcomed? Given the tone of the rest of this scroll, surely Naomi hopes that she is sending them to a place like the mother's house in the Song of Songs. In the story of Rebecca and Isaac, we find that "the girl ran to her mother's house and told them what had happened" (Gen. 24:28). Shortly thereafter, her mother and her brother agree to her marriage with a stranger, but the Bible records their strong reluctance to part with Rebecca. They plead with the messenger, "'Let the maiden remain with us some ten days, then you may go'" (Gen. 24:55). The courtship ends in the tent of the lover: "Isaac brought her into the tent [house] of his mother Sarah, and he took Rebecca as his wife. Isaac loved her, and thus found comfort after his mother's death" (Gen. 24:67). The mother's houses in Genesis are similar to those in the Song of Songs. In sum, although the term "mother's house" appears only four times in the Bible, in every case it seems to be a welcoming place where the daughter is cherished.

In addition to the two appearances of "mother's house," the word "mother" appears in the Song of Songs five times—a high proportion for any book of the Bible[37]—while the words "father" and "father's house" do not appear at all in this scroll. Twice we hear of the mother of the daughter's brothers, twice of the mother of a male lover, and three times of the mother of the daughter. Altogether, "mother" is used once by the lover, once by an anonymous speaker, and five times by the daughter. It is the daughter who twice speaks of "my mother's house," who twice identifies her brothers as "my mother's sons" (1:6, 8:1), and who imagines her lover's conception thus: "It was there your mother conceived you, / There she who bore you conceived you" (8:5). If the mother is in this scroll, she is there through the agency of the daughter. Just as in the scroll of Ruth, the fate of the daughter forces us to pay attention to the mother.

The similarities between Ruth and the Song of Songs do not end here, however. Just as the extraordinarily loving relationship between Ruth and Naomi seems to spill over into all of the relationships in the scroll of Ruth, the excess of love in the Song of Songs permeates every relationship. The daughter clearly cherishes her mother and the mother of her lover, and even though she may initially describe her brothers as dictatorial—"My mother's sons were angry with me, / They made me watch the vineyards" (1:6)—she later tells her lover that they could kiss in the street. "If only it could be as with a brother, / As if you had nursed at my mother's breast" (8:1). Here and in 8:8–9, the brothers come across as zealous yet devoted guardians with whom she does not always agree. In another section of the scroll, an anonymous speaker tells the maidens of Zion to "go forth / And gaze upon King Solomon / Wearing the crown that his mother / Gave him on his wedding day" (3:11). Here the mother, not the father, plays an active role on her son's wedding day.[38]

Throughout the Song of Songs, the lover praises the daughter extravagantly. He makes comparisons to flora that we now find commonplace as well as architectural comparisons and faunal metaphors that are now odd.[39] In the context of the Bible, his praise in 6:9 is just as startling as such expressions as "your neck is like the tower of David" or "your hair is as a flock of goats" (4:4) because he speaks of the preciousness of the daughter to her mother.[40] The narrators of the biblical text do not prepare us for such a mother-daughter relationship. The mother in the Song of Songs has sons and this daughter, but the idiom indicates not only that she prizes the daughter but that she treasures the daughter *over* the sons. Ariel and Chana Bloch point out that "one she is to her mother" (Song of Songs 6:9) shows "a child's unique belovedness or preciousness,"[41] but it is worth emphasizing only in the Song of Songs is this idiom applied to a daughter.[42]

CONCLUSION

The Bible contains only a scattering of mother-daughter relationships, and one may easily move over them, not taking account of the deep and powerful relationships found within. Once analyzed, however, they emerge as unexpectedly and movingly positive stories of care and devotion. And they add another dimension to our study of biblical motherhood. They form a continuum with the imagery of God as the caring mother of Israel in exilic Isaiah. Over the ages, biblical exegesis has looked at Rebecca not as daughter but as matriarch, focused on the genealogical aspects of the *Book of Ruth*, and tended to allegorize the *Song of Songs*. In so doing, scholars overlooked and obscured many traces of the mother-daughter relationship that appear in the Bible. Biblical narrative usually constructs women in accordance with a patriarchal vision; yet the Bible provides some positive portrayals of the mother-daughter relationship. Focusing on these traces of mother and daughter in the Bible reminds us that women must have played far more varied and significant roles in the life of ancient Israel than the textual evidence leads us to believe.[43] There are many gaps in our knowledge about ancient women, but not everything about their lives is missing. The biblical mother-daughter relationship, as I have shown, is an enduring element in the Bible well worth recovering.

NOTES

1. The exegesis of the rabbis on this point is telling. See b. *Baba Bathra* 16b on Genesis 24.1: "[It is written,] *The Lord had blessed Abraham in all things* [*ba-kol*]. What is meant by '*in all things*'? R. Meir said: In the fact that he had no daughter; R. Judah said: In the fact that he had a daughter. Others say that Abraham had a daughter whose name was "*ba-kol*," suggesting that every quality was contained in her.

2. I discuss here the Tamar of 2 Samuel, who is the daughter of King David and Maacah, not the Tamar of Genesis 38, who is the daughter-in-law of Judah and the mother of his twin sons, Perez and Zerah.

3. For example, see Barbara Bakke Kaiser, "Poet as 'Female Impersonator': The Image of Daughter Zion as Speaker in Biblical Poems of Suffering," *Journal of Religion*, no. 67 (1987): 164–82. Kaiser demonstrates how the biblical poets used female experience as a metaphor to express joy or agony over Jerusalem's fate or to give voice to other happy or painful experiences of the nation. Barbara Bakke Kaiser uses the word *bat* in a precise, carefully defined sense, quoting William Lanahan's definition given in a study of the book of Lamentations. On the word *bat*, see also *Encyclopedia Judaica*, 16: 161, s.v. "virgin, virginity." A. Even-Shoshan, *A New Concordance of the Old Testament* (Jerusalem, Israel: Kiryath Sepher, 1985); Robert Young, *Analytical Concordance to the Bible* (Grand Rapids, Michigan: William B. Eerdmans, 1970), s.v. "daughter" and "son."

4. There are many more, of course, but it seems unnecessary to go into them all here, as they all serve essentially the same function. See Young (1970) for complete list.

5. See, for example, Isaiah 1:8 for daughter/Israel abandoned; 2 Kings 19:21 and Isaiah 37:22 for daughter scorning enemies of Israel; Isaiah 3:16 for daughters as vain; Lamentations 1:6, 8–9 for fallen Israel figured as daughter/harlot. In the Bible, women seem to play a prominent role in mourning rituals (e.g., Isaiah 15:2, 32:11–12; Jeremiah 7:29, 9:17, 16:6, 41:5, 47:5, 48:37; Micah 1:16) and in rituals of celebration (e.g., Judges 21:16–24; Isaiah 5:1–7).

6. Karla G. Shargent comes to the same conclusion from a different starting point: "Contrary to the gender assumptions of the public/private dichotomy, which would confine daughters to the private sphere, the narrative daughters of the Hebrew Bible are remarkably mobile and can be found in the most disparate locations." See her "Living on the Edge: The Liminality of Daughters in Genesis to 2 Samuel," in *A Feminist Companion to Samuel and Kings*, ed. Athalya Brenner (Sheffield, England: Sheffield Academic Press, 1994), 40.

7. For more on this topic, see Chapter 6, "The Motherly Role of God in the Bible."

8. We briefly make note here; a fuller discussion will follow in chapter 6.

9. Jeremiah 51:5, "For Israel and Judah were not widowed [*'alman*] / Of their God the Lord of Hosts," is the exception to this rule. Many commentators change the reading of the text from *'alman* (widower) to *'almanah* (widow) to prevent the possibility of figuring God as the wife with the people as his husband. In "widow" there is still a certain distancing of the sexual.

10. For example, Exodus 20:12, 21:15, 21:17; Deuteronomy 5:16; Leviticus 19:3, 20:9; Proverbs 1:8, 6:20, 20:20.

11. The role of the queen mother (*gevirah*) at court is perhaps an exception in that the king's mother may have held an official position as an advisor to her son. On this see, for example, Niels-Erik A. Andreasen, "The Role of the Queen Mother in Israelite Society," *Catholic Biblical Quarterly*, no. 45 (1983): 179–94; Zafrira Ben-Barak, "The Status and Right of the *Gebira*," *Journal of Biblical Literature*, no. 110 (1991): 23–34. See chapter 6 for a more detailed study of the *gevirah*, the Queen Mother.

12. Carol Meyers argues that "women in agrarian household settings probably exercised some control over the marital arrangements of their offspring. The Bible calls the household 'mother's household' rather than the usual 'father's household' in several passages concerned with marriageable daughters (Genesis 24:28; Ruth 1:8; Song 3:4, 8:2)." See Carol L. Meyers, "Everyday Life: Women in the Period of the Hebrew Bible,'" in *The Women's Bible Commentary*, edited by Carol A. Newsom and Sharon H. Riggs, (Louisville, Kentucky: Westminster/John Knox, 1992), 249.

13. The rabbis identify the daughter of Pharaoh with Bithiah mentioned in 1 Chronicles 4:18. The Midrash comments that her name indicates that she was a daughter of God (*bat-Yah*) and celebrates her defiance to her father. See *Leviticus Rab.* 1:3.

14. Amram's name appears thirteen times in the Bible and Jochebed's twice—all in the context of genealogical lists.

15. Eileen Schuller, "Women of the Exodus in the Biblical Retellings of the Second Temple Period in *Gender and Difference in Ancient Israel*, ed. by. P.Day (Minneapolis: Fortress Press, 1989). Also, see my book, *From Eve to Esther*, in which I speak of the midwives, in addition to Miriam and Pharaoh's daughter.

16. Eileen Schuller, " Women of the Exodus in Biblical Retellings of the Second Temple Period," in *Gender and Difference in Ancient Israel*, ed. Peggy L. Day, (Minneapolis, Minnesota: Fortress Press, 1989); J. Cheryl Exum, "'You Shall Let Every Daughter Live': A Study of Exodus 1.8–2.10," *Semeia*, no. 28 (1983): 63–82. More ambivalent views about the roles of the women of Exodus can be found in, for example, J. Cheryl Exum, "'Mothers in Israel': A Familiar Story Reconsidered," in *Feminist Interpretation of the Bible*, ed. Letty M. Russell, (Philadelphia, Pennsylvania: Westminster, 1985); Drorah O'Donnell Setel, "Exodus," in *The Women's Bible Commentary*, eds. Carol A. Newsom and Sharon H. Ringe, (Louisville, Kentucky: Westminster/John Knox, 1992).

17. Susan Niditch, "Genesis," in *The Women's Bible Commentary*, ed. Carol A. Newsom and Sharon H. Riggs (Louisville, Kentucky.: Westminster/John Knox, 1992), 23.

18. Later, Simeon is chosen, from among the ten of Jacob's sons who went for food to the land of Egypt, as the brother who is left with Joseph as a hostage for their

return with Benjamin, Joseph's brother (Genesis 42). Is this because Simeon is a troublemaker? Because Joseph would find him easiest to kill? Because his brothers or his father will miss him most or least? It is impossible to tell from the narrative. Note also that Leah does not intercede for Simeon and Levi, which might indicate that she supported or that she was appalled by their response to their sister's rape. Of course, she may have died before this point in the biblical narrative.

19. Interestingly, the rabbis spend some time developing Dinah's relationship to Leah and discussing her fate. For example, they suggest that by going out alone, Dinah is imitating her mother's behavior ("Like mother, like daughter," they quote), and they marry her off variously to Job or her brother Simeon. See Leila Bronner, *From Eve to Esther: Rabbinic Reconstructions of Biblical Women* (Louisville, Kentucky: Westminster/John Knox, 1994), 118–22.

20. See Anita Diamant, *The Red Tent* (New York: Picador 1997), a midrashic novel about the life of Dina.

21. *Genesis Rab.* 80:3; Avivah Gottlieb Zornberg, *Genesis: The Beginning of Desire* (Philadelphia, Pennsylvania: Jewish Publication Society, 1995), 225–29.

22. See, for example, Ganse Little, "2 Samuel: Exposition," in *The Interpreter's Bible*, 6 vols. (Nashville, Tennessee: Abingdon, 1952–1956), 2: 1113.

23. *Sanhedrin* 21a.

24. Ben Sira 7:24–25, 22:3–5 (2nd century B.C.E.) reiterates the lack of warmth and closeness in father and daughter relationships; W. C. Trenchard, "Woman as Daughter," in *Ben Sira's View of Women: A Literary Analysis*, Brown Judaic Studies 38, ed. Jacob Neusner (Chico, California: Scholars Press, 1982).

25. See Phyllis Trible, *Texts of Terror: Literary-Feminist Readings of Biblical Narratives* (Philadelphia, Pennsylvania: Fortress Press, 1984), 53–54: "David's anger signifies complete sympathy for Amnon and total disregard for Tamar. How appropriate that the story never refers to David and Tamar as father and daughter! The father identifies with the son; the adulterer supports the rapist; the male has joined male to deny justice for the female."

26. Rivkah Harris, "Independent Women in Ancient Mesopotamia?" in *Women's Earliest Records from Ancient Egypt and Western Asia*, ed. Barbara S. Lesko (Atlanta, Georgia: Scholars Press, 1989), 153, similarly notes in passing the way brothers play a protective role for their sisters.

27. The narrator carefully distinguishes that Ruth and Orpah are daughters-in-law and that Naomi is "mother-in-law"; Boaz, too, notes that Naomi is Ruth's "mother-in-law." Naomi calls Ruth and Orpah "daughters," Boaz and Naomi both call Ruth "daughter," but Ruth calls Boaz only "my lord."

28. We find such scenes in Ruth, the Song of Songs, and perhaps in Genesis 24, when Rebecca runs home to "her mother's house." Lot's daughters cooperate in seducing their father, and Jephthah's daughter is comforted by her female companions. In the Bible there are also scenes of cruelty between women as they compete for children (e.g., Sarah and Hagar, Leah and Rachel, Hannah and Peninah). It must be significant that, as will be discussed below, the three stories of cross-generational affection between women include the term "mother's house."

29. See Ruth 2:20.

30. See Edward F. Campbell, Jr., *Ruth*, Anchor Bible, vol. 7 (New York: Doubleday, 1975), 6; Robert Gordis, "Love, Marriage, and Business in the Book of Ruth: A Chapter in Hebrew Customary Law," In *Light Unto My Path: Old Testament Studies in Honor of Jacob M. Myers*, ed. H.N. Bream, R. D. Heim, and C.A. Moore (Philadelphia: Temple University Press, 1974).

31. Compare the words of Elkanah to his barren wife Hannah: "'Am I not better, do I not mean [*tov*] more to you than ten sons?'" (1 Samuel 1:8). See Edward F. Campbell Jr., *Ruth, The Anchor Bible*, no. 15 (New York: Doubleday, 1975), 164, on the uses of *tov* in the book of Ruth to emphasize "not only Ruth's quality of person but also her prime importance to Naomi's well-being."

32. Ariel Bloch and Chana Bloch, *The Song of Songs: A New Translation with an Introduction and Commentary* (New York: Random House, 1995), 6.

33. We discuss Dinah and Tamar as two humiliated and wounded women, but there are two other daughters, mentioned by name, but not discussed in this book, who are victims of violence, namely, Jephthah's daughter and the Levite's concubine.

34. The association of the mother and the mother's house with learning appears as well in Ruth (who learns from Naomi) and in Proverbs (Woman Wisdom, chaps. 1–9; praise of woman, 31:10–31; and passim).

35. For this reading and the wide range of allegorical and sociological interpretations that the term "mother's house" has received, see M. H. Pope, *Song of Songs* (Garden City, New York: Doubleday, 1977), 421–22.

36. See the article by Carol Meyers addressing the sociological implications of this term and drawing out the similarities of its context in "'To Her Mother's House': Considering a Counterpart to the Israelite *bêt 'ab*," in *The Bible and the Politics of Exegesis*, edited by David Jobling, Peggy L. Day, and Gerald T. Sheppard (Cleveland, Ohio: Pilgrim Press, 1991), 39–51. Meyers also discusses the history of emendation that tends to regard "mother's house" as a textual corruption. See also Pope (1977), 421–22; Carol Meyers, "Returning Home: Ruth 1.8 and the Gendering of the Book of Ruth" in *A Feminist Companion to Ruth*, ed. Athalya Brenner (Sheffield, England: Sheffield Academic Press, 1993).

37. "Mother" appears 209 times in the Hebrew Bible, "mother-in-law" 11 times (10 in Ruth, 1 in Micah; see also Deuteronomy 27:23).

38. For another discussion of King Solomon's wedding, see "Chapter 3: Queen Mothers and Wise Women."

39. Particularly good on the latter is Carol Meyers, "Gender Imagery in the Song of Songs," *Hebrew Annual Review*, no. 10 (1986): 209–23.

40. Naming a daughter "Hephzibah," which means "my delight is in her," indicates a warm feeling for the daughter but the Bible does not provide substantiating details; see 2 Kings 21:1 (the wife of Hezekiah and the mother of Manasseh, king of Judah) and Isaiah 62:4 (a name for Jerusalem restored). The description of the warmth among women here in the Song of Songs is as unique as the warmth between mother and daughter.

41. See Bloch and Bloch *The Song of Songs* (New York: Random House, 1995), 190.

42. Compare Genesis 22:2 and Proverbs 4:3.

43. J. Cheryl Exum, *Fragmented Women: Feminist (Sub)versions of Biblical Narratives* (Valley Forge, Pennsylvania: Trinity Press International, 1993), 136.

Chapter Five

The Metaphorical Mother

. . . you arose a mother in Israel.

Judges 5:7

Where there is a mother in the house matters speed well.

AMOS BRONSON ALCOTT, *Table Talk: Nurture*

Motherhood is often associated with acts of creating, caring, and counseling, as we have demonstrated in the previous chapters. The mothers discussed thus far are biological mothers who boldly influence the private sector (chapters 1–2, 4) or public domain (chapter 3) through the raising and caring for their offspring. We turn our attention now from biological mothers to another category of motherhood, which we would like to designate the "metaphorical mother." What constitutes a biological mother is clear enough, but what do we mean by metaphorical mother? The term metaphor implies the use of an analogy to imaginatively identify one thing with another. In using the term "metaphorical mother," we emphasize the "mothering" that several biblical women do on an overtly communal level. These "mothers" nurture a population of symbolic, rather than biological children. The text does not present these women as giving birth to literal children (although they very well may have been biological mothers), but they contribute much to the birth and growth of a budding nation. These symbolic mothers play a crucial role in the advancement of their people. They are administrators of God's plans, protectors of the community, and givers of wise and much needed counsel at momentous points in Israel's history.

We first focus on Deborah, who remains the best biblical example of a metaphorical mother. Significantly she is the only woman to bear the title, "mother in Israel,"[1] although she most frequently is characterized as a prophet and judge. As the only explicitly signified "mother in Israel" she operates as a paradigm by which we can view other female leaders of the Bible. Deborah is the metaphorical mother *par excellence*, and by examining her character we believe we find other women who possess similar traits and who can likewise be categorized as metaphorical mothers. After discussing Deborah,[2] we then study Miriam and Esther, who seem to operate in a like manner to Deborah, leading their people valiantly during times of prosperity and joy, calamity and disaster. Miriam, along with her brothers, leads the Israelites through their desert wanderings and gives poetic expression to the Israelite victory over the Egyptian army. Esther valiantly and courageously represents her people to a pagan king, and self-sacrificially lays her own life on the line to preserve the Jewish people.

We then move our discussion to women who are less influential, but who nonetheless, seem to qualify as metaphorical mothers, owing to the roles they played in Israelite history. Although this final group of women takes up only a few brief pages in Israel's literary record, they nevertheless leave a significant mark. We first discuss the prophetess Huldah, who was sought out to provide direction, guidance and encouragement when Judah was at a theological crossroad. Secondly, we look at Rahab, a harlot, who saves her family and aids the Israelites as they enter the land. Finally, we talk about the Witch of Endor, who gives advice to King Saul, conjures up Samuel the prophet, and provides comfort and nourishment during the misguided king's hour of need. We must mention that the last three examples are ordered according to how well they fit into the paradigm of metaphorical mother, and not according to chronological order.

DEBORAH

Most readers of the Bible know Deborah as a significant prophet and judge in ancient Israel; we argue that her role as mother is likewise important. The title, "mother in Israel," has not been stressed enough when discussing the career of Deborah and we wish to highlight this aspect of her leadership.

When we read of the exploits of Deborah in Judges 4, we first see her not as a mother, but rather as a prophet and judge who leads Israel. The book of Judges describes the Israelite leaders as physically strong but spiritually weak. Locked in a series of territorial disputes with the nations around them, they are often inclined to leave the Israelite God for other gods. Because of the incompetence of the male leaders during various time periods allows strong female personalities to appear and fill the void. One by-product of the chaos of the premonarchical age is the public participation of women in the political affairs and wars of the nation. According to Judges 4, God raises up Deborah to bring a sense of order and help his people return to the ways of righteousness.

The narrators of the text describe Deborah as presiding over an administrative area extending from Ramah to Bethel. As the text relates, "Deborah . . . led Israel at that time. She used to sit under the Palm of Deborah, between Ramah and Bethel in the hill country of Ephraim, and the Israelites would come to her for decisions" (Judges 4:4,5). She receives word from God ("the Lord, the God of Israel has commanded," [v.6]), and delivers the divine instructions.[3] She is the only female judge, and the only judge to share the office of both prophet and judge. Deborah commandeers a defensive war against Israel's enemy in which her role is paramount: the fighter Barak will not lead the Israelites against the Canaanites unless Deborah joins them in battle. Barak's insistence that Deborah participate demonstrates that her contribution must have been considered invaluable. When she accedes, she becomes the flame that ignites the Israelites' fire.[4]

Reading the poetry of Judges 5, we are presented with a different portrait of Deborah. Surprisingly she is introduced as "mother in Israel." While Judges 4 focuses on Deborah's role as prophet and judge, the epic poem in the next chapter offers a new image of Deborah as Mother. She still retains her leadership abilities of the prose account, but nowhere does the song call her judge or prophet! Instead, she is portrayed as a person of authority under the rubric of mother. As noted by de Boer, Deborah has great power and "as a mother she gives the just decision from which life or death depends."[5] Frymer-Kensky also takes notice of Deborah's motherly authority, noticing that mothers might attain political prominence and even suggesting that the term "mother" was perhaps an honorific.[6] Why does Deborah call herself mother (if she indeed authored the poem), and how did future faith communities understand her role as a mother in Israel?

The epic starts by quoting words attributed to Deborah in the form of a song. Deborah says, "I will sing, I will make melody to the LORD of Israel." Then the poem follows with a description of a time of political and social upheaval in Israel's history. In the days of the judges when anarchy reigned because there was no centralized monarchy, people were afraid to journey on the main roads, lest they fell under attack by marauding bands. As verse 6 expresses, ". . . caravans ceased, and wayfarers went by roundabout paths. Deliverance ceased." The need for a leader to bring order and security is obvious. The song then dramatically introduces the figure of Deborah: "Until you arose, O Deborah, arose a mother in Israel."[7] Deborah wielded greater control over the tribes of Israel for the forty years that she was in power than any other male judge before or after her. Deborah arrives on the scene as a savior figure who succeeds in uniting her people, and who finally delivers her people from fear and devastation.

In literary sources that discuss the Song of Deborah, we have not found that emphasis is put on the mother in Israel image; instead, most commentators highlight her role as prophet and judge. One ancient commentator who draws upon her role as mother is Pseudo-Philo, a document that is part of the Pseudepigrapha. He imagines Deborah delivering her last command upon her deathbed: "Listen now, my people. Behold I am warning you as a woman of God and am enlightening you as one from the female race; and obey me like your mother and heed my words. . . ."[8] According to Pseudo-Philo the mother is an important symbol for the roles, both military and civil, that Deborah assumes on behalf of her people. Pseudo-Philo highlights Deborah's role as mother, which perhaps indicates that in his mind her position as mother was equal to her position as prophet and judge. He assumes that she can exercise great power as a mother, and his comments reflect our position that mothers possessed unassigned authority in ancient Israel. Judges 5 portrays Deborah as a mother and leader, which demonstrates that her prominence stemmed not only from her role as prophet and judge, but also from her role as mother. In reading Judges 5, we see that the title "mother," in and of itself carried great authority.

Rabbinic sources also comment on Deborah's function as mother. However unlike Pseudo-Philo, the rabbis do not take the positive position concerning Deborah's role as mother. Hillel, first century rabbi, noted the statement that Deborah "arose as mother in Israel" shows she was arrogant and boastful, cardinal sins in rabbinic thought. Deborah's later words in the poem, "awake, utter a song," further demonstrate, according to the rabbis, that her prophecy departed because of her pride. On the other hand, many rabbis laud her as a prophetess. For instance, *Tanna Debe Eliyahu* maintains Deborah's story illustrates that the spirit of the Lord rests upon individuals according to their merit rather than their gender.[9] *Targum Jonathan* elaborates upon the Song of Deborah,[10] in which one midrash even considers her song as turning night into day. Although motherhood is a prescribed role in rabbinic thought, and even the ideal role for women, the rabbis surprisingly do not pick up on the title the Judges 5 poem gives to Deborah, "mother in Israel," and only use the statement to criticize a woman leader.

We claim that Deborah's role as mother is a very significant one, perhaps as significant as her role as prophet or judge. In the epic poetry she is a mother in Israel, and a powerful figure of influence in the triumph of the Israelites over the Canaanites. In Judges 4, she has an important position, but perhaps more of a supporting role. The Israelites consult her in private, and when Barak approaches her he does so without an audience present. In contrast, in the poetic version, she leads publicly, and importantly, as a mother in Israel. Although we obviously cannot get into the mind of Deborah to understand how she herself defined "mother in Israel," the narrator seemed to use the phrase as a way to describe her leadership, indicating that, "Mother," was an authoritative title.

In sum, Deborah emerges as a metaphorical mother. Deborah does not sling stones, wield swords, or thrust spears; instead, she empowers her people with her words, and in this way, she acts as a paradigm for other female leaders. When women leaders "mother" their people, they do so most often through persuasive words. They offer encouragement, give prophecies, and sing songs. Frymer-Kensky notes, "Like Moses, Deborah is not a battle commander. Her role is to inspire, predict, and celebrate in song. Her weapon is the word, and her very name is an anagram of 'she spoke.'"[11] Deborah uses her way with words to wield influence in the public realm. Biblical characters often live out some aspect of the meaning behind their names and Deborah was no exception. Frymer-Kensky explains, "the fullest sense of Deborah is revealed in her name . . . which is a noun meaning 'bee.' This name may hint at the fullest sense of her as 'mother in Israel.' Like the queen bee, she raises up the swarm for battle, sending out the drones to protect the hive and conquer new territory."[12] Deborah's real weapon of strength is her mind. And in this way the mothers of the Bible are all woven together: their ability to think and to reason allows them to manipulate circumstances and exert influence within their social realm. Though not as physically strong as their male counterparts, biblical mothers operate with great mental acuity and strength.

FEMALE LEADERS AS METAPHORICAL MOTHERS

We have looked at Deborah as a metaphorical mother *par excellence*, and turn our attention to other female leaders who seem to exhibit similar mothering qualities. We hypothesize now whether these other examples could be acting as surrogate mothers on a metaphorical level. We suggest that although the following women are not given the epithet of "mother," nor presented in the text as biological mothers, they emerge as symbolic mothers through their actions. When they lead their people, they seem to do so by caring for, nurturing, counseling, and in short, by "mothering" them. These women are connected in that they come onto the scene during momentous events within Israelite history. They appear in times of national rebirth and times of national crisis. They differ from biological mothers in the obvious sense that they have not given birth to literal children, at least the narrators do not portray them as such, yet they influence a far wider audience than biological mothers, affecting their ethnic group, or even a whole nation. We now want to explore the characters Miriam, Rehab, the Witch of Endor, Huldah and Esther to see whether these women qualify as metaphorical mothers.

MIRIAM

To mention Miriam in connection with the topic of motherhood may at first seem surprising and even ironic. Nowhere does the Bible state or hint that Miriam was married or had children.[13] We discuss her here because she emerges as a figure who possesses many mothering qualities. In this way, we understand her as a national mother, concerned with the welfare of her people. We will survey the seven biblical references to Miriam and create an image of Miriam, not only as a prophet and leader, but also as a candidate for possible national motherhood.

Miriam first appears as the unnamed sister of Moses, who leads the Egyptian princess to Moses' biological mother for use as a wet nurse (Ex.2:1–10). As the older sibling, Miriam acts as sort of a mother-figure to her younger brother. She materializes as an active force in molding his early life. As Frymer-Kensky notes, "Moses is born, and saved to be reborn, by the collaboration of a triad of daughters, who begin the redemption of Israel." She groups Yochebed, Miriam, and the daughter of Pharaoh together as co-mothers in Moses' upbringing.[14] Miriam, though not a biological mother, rightly belongs in this triad, according to Frymer-Kensky. Miriam is an acting agent of motherhood.

She is also the first woman to bear the title, "prophet." She therefore becomes an archetype in the female prophetic tradition, just as Moses heads the male archetype (Deut. 34:10). Miriam, however, does not seem to play the role of prophetic figure. As Brenner states, "no hint as to the nature of Miriam's prophetic activity has been preserved in biblical sources."[15] However, Miriam can be viewed as a prophet through her use of liturgical song to express Israel's past triumph over the Egyptians. She gives expression to the redemptive acts of God, and can be viewed in the same vein as many of the literary prophets who tell of God's deeds through poetry.

Though the biblical text does not mention husband or children in connection with Miriam, in her role as national leader she embodies many traits that typify a mother. She is a vibrant and encouraging source of strength to her people in their time of joyous victory. As the book of Judges does for Deborah, the book of Exodus records a poem in Miriam's honor: "Then Miriam the prophet, Aaron's sister, took a timbrel in her hand, and all the women went out after her in dance with timbrels. . . ." (Exodus 15:20). Miriam's exuberance inspired other women to sing in joy, inspiring the people and radiating the happiness of the entire community. It is noteworthy that the Bible portrays Miriam, along with Moses, as articulating, through ritual song and dance, the religious dimension of Israel's exodus from Egypt. The depiction of the head male and female leaders of Israel together praising God for his deliverance of the children of Israel makes for a striking image.

Miriam is as much a leader to her people as her brothers, Moses and Aaron. As God's spirit rests upon Moses, so the text also acknowledges that Miriam and Aaron are co-leaders to Moses. The prophet Micah records God speaking of the deliverance of his people: "I brought you up from the land of Egypt, I redeemed you from the house of bondage, and I sent before you Moses, Aaron, and Miriam" (6:4). This verse highlights Miriam's role as metaphorical mother. Along with her male counterparts, she was used by God as an agent for divine deliverance. She is the nurturing female figure in the triad of Israel's leaders.

Like any human leader, Miriam had flaws. Though she interacted with God, experienced his presence, and conveyed God's actions through song, she also spoke against Moses concerning his Cushite wife (Numbers 12:1). Though we will not discuss this unhappy story at length, because it does not relate to the subject at hand, we mention it briefly for it demonstrates the great love of the children of Israel for Miriam. Despite the instructions of God and Moses the people refuse to continue their march in the wilderness until their beloved Miriam is restored to health (Numbers 12:15). She was punished by God for her slight, but the great love and affection of her people gave them a sense of loyalty and compassion for her in her time of punishment. Surely this expression of mutual loyalty shows that Miriam had a maternal, loving relationship with her people. The Israelites great love for her compelled them to remain by her side, even though Moses and God had commanded them to move on. The people feel a sense of protectiveness toward her, as one would toward one's own mother (Num. 12:15).

Interestingly, though the Bible rarely records a woman's demise, Miriam's death is recorded by the biblical writers (Num.20:2). Immediately following the verse about her death, the text announces that, "the community was without water." Talmudic rabbis make a connection between Miriam's death and the subsequent lack of water (*b. Ta'an* 9a). As long as Miriam was alive, writes the exegete Rashi (quoting from *Ta'anit 9a*), the people were provided, in her merit, with a well of water that followed them wherever they went. Immediately upon Miriam's death, however, the well vanishes. The people are so frustrated by the lack of water that they envy their brethren who are already dead. Because of her merit the children of Israel received water. Thus at her death, the Israelites experienced loss of the divine supply, which had to be renegotiated. Miriam's connection to water, a substance necessary for human survival, suggests that she was crucial to the wellbeing of the community. In short, Miriam, just as a mother, was a life source to her symbolic children.

ESTHER

Esther, along with Miriam and Deborah, appears as a unique figure in biblical tradition, for she, like the others, can be viewed as a significant national leader in her own right. Deborah is called "mother" because of her authority and leadership not only as judge and prophet but also as a mother in Israel. Similarly, Miriam is a mother figure because of the special relationship she forges with her people. Esther, too, uses her political position to defend the lives of her people just as a protective mother would save the lives of her children.

The story of Esther is traditionally interpreted as the tale of a beautiful but passive queen, but this is an incomplete assessment of Esther. If she at first appears as stereotypically feminine, malleable and docile, she certainly grows and develops, and becomes a strong leader ready to sacrifice herself for the safety of her community. In her selfless commitment to her people, she is a mother figure. Her courage and understated political skill exercised within the ambit of the autocratic court of King Ahasuerus, propel her into the position of national hero and political mother of the Jewish people.

The story of Esther is placed in the Persian royal court in approximately 485–465 BCE. While scholarly studies of the book of Esther concentrate on its historical placement, its provenance, its canonicity, and on such issues as the absence of God's name and the general dearth of religious references, I find most noteworthy as well as unusual Esther's leadership role as metaphorical mother.[16] The basic premise of Esther's story is well known. The following synopsis, however, reflects my interpretation that sets Esther among the other women leaders who are great metaphorical mothers and nation-builders.

The narrative begins by describing Esther as a beautiful girl being moved around by the will of powerful men. After Ahasuerus' dismissal of Queen Vashti (1:12–22) at the behest of his (possibly drunken) advisors, a search for a new queen is undertaken by Ahasuerus' servants (2:2–4). Esther, an orphan who has been raised by her uncle Mordecai, is taken to the palace (2:8). She greatly pleases Hegai, the king's eunuch in charge of the harem, who provides her with the best of everything (2:9). Esther does not reveal her Jewish ancestry because Mordecai has forbidden her to do so (2:10, 20). When Esther goes to the king, she finds favor in his eyes, and he makes her queen in place of Vashti. The king throws a banquet in Esther's honor, calling it "the banquet of Esther" (2:17–18). Ironically, an orphan girl possesses no mother is a role model and will eventually develop into a national mother, caring for her surrogate children, and acting as a savior to the Jewish people.

Once inside the court of the king, Esther finds herself in a precarious position. She uses her wits to come up with a plan of manipulation. Mordecai suggests that she approach the king to plea on behalf of her people. At first she refuses, since her life would be at risk. However, Esther, utilizing her womanly intuition and wisdom, comes up with her own plan of action. She finally decides to go before the king, putting her life on the line for her beloved people, to invite him to a banquet. She decides to throw a series of banquets, choosing to use food as a means to influence the king and destroy Haman. During the second banquet she reveals her true identity as a Jewess and pleads like a devoted mother to save her people from the destruction planned by Haman. She then goes before the throne of the king asking for mercy on behalf of her surrogate children, the Jewish people.

Esther's last two actions in the Scroll are unquestionably those of a national leader. She requests that the king grant "to the Jews that are in Shushan to do tomorrow also according unto this day's decree, and let Haman's ten sons be hanged upon the gallows" (9:13). By this request, Esther makes sure that the people of the king's capital know that the lives of the Jews are not to be taken lightly, as Haman had done. She also institutes, with Mordecai, the festival of Purim. Mordecai writes the first letter to the Jews, but it is the second letter written by Esther and issued on her own authority as queen that establishes the festival for all time.

> Then Queen Esther daughter of Abigail wrote a second letter of Purim for the purpose of confirming with full authority the aforementioned one of Mordecai the Jew. . . . These days of Purim shall be observed at their proper time, as Mordecai the Jew—and now Queen Esther—has obligated them to do . . . And Esther's ordinance validating these observances of Purim was recorded in a scroll (9:29–32).[17]

In no other story does the Bible attest to a woman's sponsoring a written tradition or establishing the observance of a festival.[18] As national mother, Esther establishes a significant Jewish tradition that would prevail over centuries and continue to define her people long after her death.

The Talmud highlights Esther's role as sponsor and founder of the festival of Purim. The rabbis narrate that Esther sends them a letter requesting that they perpetuate her name, book, and festival for all time: "Write me down for future generations."[19] She argues her case by stating that she was already recorded in the annals of the Persians, and now wishes to be remembered by her own people for her role in their redemption. Seeking scriptural validation before agreeing, the sages find it by reinterpreting the biblical verse: "Inscribe this in a document as a reminder," (Exod 17:14) which refers to the war against Amalek.[20] The rabbis yield to her wish and allow her story to be hallowed. This talmudic reference echoes the biblical account cited above of Esther's desire for posterity (Esth 9:29f). It is the only context in which the rabbis choose a biblical woman to serve as the catalyst for the writing down of an oral tradition and, by so doing, solidify Esther's standing as a matriarchal ancestor. Esther came into a position of power and influence, much like her biblical predecessors, Deborah and Miriam, during a time of social and political turmoil for the Jewish people. Perhaps her participation was ostensibly the result of Persian custom, but we prefer to see in the case of Esther a discernible tendency for leaders to arise during times of crisis and answer to the need of the people. Mordecai, by calling upon Esther to approach the king and subsequently to save her people, helps catapult Esther into national motherhood. Because she plays a central role in the deliverance of her people, the biblical scroll *(megillah)* about Purim is thus named for Esther. In the final analysis, Esther serves as a metaphorical mother, who establishes a cultural precedent for her symbolic children, the Jewish people.

THREE SURPRISING METAPHORICAL MOTHERS?

Above we discussed Deborah, Miriam, and Esther, prominent communal leaders, who, we were able to demonstrate, also acted as metaphorical mothers. The motherly traits of the women whom we study below are not immediately perceptible. Our study demonstrates that Huldah the Prophet, Rahab the Harlot, and the Witch of Endor can be viewed in a similar light as Deborah, Miriam and Esther. That is, they possess qualities and behave in ways that allow us to categorize them as metaphorical mothers.

HULDAH

We first focus on Huldah the Prophet. Huldah's account is found in 2 Kings 22:14–20 and 2 Chronicles 34:11–28.[21] She was the wife of Shallum, keeper of the wardrobe, and a temple prophet who delivered oracles. Though living in a radically different time, like the above example of Esther, she gives guidance to a people in crisis, who were constantly fearing attack from their neighbors.

Huldah lived during the time of King Josiah of Judah. It was a time of much social, political, and religious change. The nation of Judah had seen the fall of its northern counterpart, Samaria, about a century earlier and wanted to avoid a similar fate. Josiah had come into power during this precarious period and he, as 1 Kings records, "did what was pleasing to the Lord and he followed all the ways of his ancestor David" (1 Ki.22:2). Evidently, part of Josiah's reforms involved the issuing of new policies regarding the practice of God's law. After a "book of the law" was found in the Temple archives, the king and his advisors saw how far the Judahites had strayed from the commandments of God. When Josiah realized the depth of wickedness that the people had fallen to, he "rent his cloths" (v.11). He then commanded his advisors to inquire of God on his own behalf and "on the behalf of the people, and on behalf of all of Judah." The king, wanting to know if future demise was imminent, and seeking to find a solution to what he saw as certain destruction, sought out help from the prophet, Huldah. Interestingly, a woman, a maternal figure, offers guidance to an entire people. We conjecture that Josiah consulted a female prophet because of the influence of his godly mother, Jedidah[22] daughter of Adaiah, who hailed from the pious hill country of Judah.[23] Huldah provided wisdom and direction, delivering an oracle of mingled judgment and mercy, during a time of great turmoil.

Huldah belongs in our discussion of metaphorical mothers because she offers comfort to a royal figure, King Josiah, and she was consulted on behalf of an entire nation. She also provides an explanation for Judah's ultimate destruction. Speaking for God, she states that Judah will suffer eventual wrath because the people have "forsaken [God] and have made offerings to other gods and vexed [God] with all their deeds" (vv.16–17). Though she does not offer comfort to the people, she presents consolation to King Josiah, mothering him in a time of national crisis and upheaval. The whole of Judah depended upon Huldah for guidance and direction. They needed to hear from God and she was the oracle-giver, delivering a message of judgment, a message oft resonated in the words of the literary prophets. Her position as prophet was a God-given role. Unlike priests, generals, judges, and governors, she was not appointed by superiors, but received her vocation by the "gift of the spirit," offered to whomever God deems fit. Motherhood and prophecy are connected since they both hail from the hand of God. Both are divinely given occupations.

God's words to Josiah come through the mouth of Huldah. She consoles him by reassuring him that he "will be laid in [his] tomb in peace" and further that [his] eyes would not see all the disaster that [God] will bring upon [Judah]" (2 Ki.22:19–20). Sometimes national mothers, much like their biological counterparts, have to be the bearers of bad news. At times they speak words of hope and encouragement, urging growth for their symbolic children, but at other times, they must communicate the harsh reality of life. Huldah is appointed by God to bring the bad tidings of Judah's eventual destruction to a royal figure. She fulfills her role, but she probably does so reluctantly. Herself an inhabitant of Judah, no doubt she felt a sense of fear and foreboding at the thought of Judah's demise. Yet Huldah does not first think of herself. She is faithful to deliver God's message as received. Further, she offers words of encouragement to Josiah—reassuring him that God will keep him from witnessing the fall of his people.

Interestingly a woman is consulted at this time of uncertainty and impending doom. Although reliance upon a woman may strike some readers as strange, the narrators of 2 Kings and 2 Chronicles are not surprised by this fact. Is this because women are instinctively more intuitive and compassionate? Later rabbinic tradition gives us insight into why the royal courtiers of Josiah would approach a woman; they believed Huldah's maternal instinct would provide kindness to a nation in trouble. The rabbis point out that a woman was consulted for guidance because she would most likely offer sympathy, as a mother would to a child during a hard time.[24] The rabbis saw women as "tender-hearted" and believed that Huldah would pray for a nation and king in great need.

Before leaving the figure of Huldah, I would like to posit that she emerges as a type of religious innovator, as are some of her other maternal counterparts. As Hannah is the patron of personal prayer, and Esther the founder of the festival of Purim, Huldah is an innovator of biblical interpretation. She is the first and only person within the Bible who interprets a scroll found in the temple. She issues in a new phase of textual analysis that will become ever more important in the Second Temple period.[25]

RAHAB

We turn now to consider Rahab, the one harlot who appears by name in the Bible, and ironically, a figure we believe can be connected to national motherhood. Rahab's story is given in the Book of Joshua (2:1–24; 6:22–25). A woman of Jericho, she is described as an *'ishah zonah*, a "harlot woman." According to Scripture, she lives within the wall of the city, that is, in the disreputable outskirts. This remark suggests that she kept a house easily available to men going in and out of the city, in the outlying quarters away from the daily life of the respectable inhabitants of the town. The spies sent by Joshua lodge at her house and when the king sends for them with harm's intent, she hides them. Thus, she betrays her own people in favor of the

Israelites. Her motivation is not clear, but she seems to act to protect her father, mother, brothers—"all her father's household"—in exchange for helping the spies to escape. Rahab and her household are in fact saved when the Israelites return, and many readers of Scripture look upon her with great favor.

Although tradition considers her to be a person of merit, why do we discuss her here, in a chapter on metaphorical mothers? After all, according to patriarchal standards she is thrice under-qualified: she is a Canaanite, a woman, and a harlot! However, when we encounter Rahab she hardly gives the impression of a harlot.[26] She is a woman of strong faith who willingly shelters and aids Israelites as they spy out the land. Rahab says, "I know that the Lord has given the country to you. . . ," showing great belief in the power of the Israelite deity. She further recounts God's great deeds, reciting an ancient Israelite tradition as proof of God's power. She thus is a woman of great faith.[27]

Rahab acts with cunning and skill. She first reassures the spies that she will hide them effectively, then exacts a promise of safety from them. She pleads, "Now, since I have shown loyalty to you, swear to me by the Lord that you in turn will show loyalty to my family" (Josh.2:12). She sacrificially puts her own life on the line to save the Israelite spies, but also acts with great wisdom and foresight, finding a way to bring deliverance to her own kin. In fact, Joshua 6:25 employs the oft-used biblical editorial remark, "until this day," which demonstrates that Rahab manages to save an entire people group for many subsequent generations. She saves her family and self, but also all their future descendents, who would become part of Israel and live in the land at the time of the conquest.

Though we are dealing with the biblical Rahab, it is instructive to note the reputation she acquires within rabbinic literature. She went on to achieve status almost as an icon in the community, or as we see it, as a metaphorical mother. According to rabbinic tradition, she becomes a proselyte and is no longer called a harlot. Several midrashim transform Rahab into a righteous person (Meg. 15a). One important midrash even lists her as a woman of valor together with twenty-one other women, including the four matriarchs, Ruth, Jael, the mother of Samson, and others. The fact that she is grouped with other mothers of the tradition gives her motherly standing. And indeed she is described favorably in the Talmud, so much so that the rabbis marry her to Joshua, the conquering hero (Meg. 14b). In the Midrash she becomes a progenitor of priests and prophets. What motivated the rabbis to refashion a biblical harlot into a mother of the righteous? While there was an attempt on the part of some commentators to "clean up" Rahab's story, as is typical in midrashic literature, some rabbinic sources maintain that she was most definitely a harlot. These "tough-minded" rabbis nonetheless come to terms with her profession and contribute to the exegetical project of attributing to her outstanding qualities. Little by little Rahab is rehabilitated or transformed in rabbinic exegesis from harlot to proselyte and, ultimately, to a suitable wife for a hero of the nation. Likewise, the New Testament puts Rahab in good standing as a righteous woman of faith. She is mentioned along side the great heroes of faith within Israel's history (Hebrews 11:31).

Rahab's is the story of an actual harlot who is so impressed by the valor of the conquering Israelites that she joins the people of Israel in their destiny and becomes the mother of priests and prophets, according to rabbinic tradition. This woman is a paradigm of courage and a symbol of self-directed, destiny-changing action. Not only does the Bible not condemn Rahab, but within tradition, her reputation is rehabilitated so thoroughly through midrashic exegesis that she is transformed into an exceptional figure—virtually a heroine of the nation.

THE NECROMANCER ("WITCH") OF ENDOR

Another candidate for national motherhood is the Necromancer of Endor. She is, like Rahab, perhaps a surprising choice for the esteemed position of national mother. Her role as necromancer demonstrates that there was an opportunity for women to have a professional role in ancient Israel.[28] She performs a type of witchcraft, a practice that had been outlawed by the king and condemned by God. The text in 1 Samuel 28 shows that the nameless woman knew of the prohibition and was frightened at the prospect of being found out.

According to the narrative, King Saul was in great despair after the invasion of Israel by the Philistines and had tried consulting God by orthodox standards of divination: through dreams, prophets and the use of the Urim. Finally in his despondency he sought out a woman diviner, who would conjure up the spirit of Samuel. Help came in the form of a medium in Endor, near the plain of Megiddo. She summons up the spirit of Samuel so that Saul could question him for guidance and receive encouragement.

In this sad tale of Saul's desperation, the Witch plays the role of compassionate helper. As Saul is laying prone, terror-struck at hearing that the Lord had become his adversary (v.15), the woman looks upon him with pity and says, "Let me set before you a bit of food. Eat, and then you will have the strength to go on your way." She then prepares an elaborate meal so that he would regain his strength and be able to continue his journey. She benevolently aids him without asking for any payment in return for her services. In this way, she is a metaphorical mother, devotedly caring for the king of Israel. The historian Josephus takes note of her kind actions, encouraging his readers to follow her model of generosity.[29] Josephus remarks, "she did not refuse him as a stranger . . . but she had compassion upon him, and comforted him, and exhorted him to what he was greatly averse to, and offered him the only creature she had, as a poor woman, and that earnestly, and with great humanity."

The Witch of Endor mothers by caring for the king of an emerging nation. Israel was at the threshold of becoming a viable kingdom, after a period of being ruled by a series of judges. Saul leads the people toward independence, but keeps experiencing defeat at the hands of the Philistines, the coastal nemesis of the children of Israel. He is at the lowest point in his career when he consults the Witch of Endor. Rather than protecting her own life, she overtly disobeys the decree of the king, practices the art of necromancy, and shows tendencies of a nurturing mother. Even after hearing from the mouth of Samuel that Saul's career is nearly over, the medium does not despise his low standing, but rather offers him all she has, spiritually and materially.

Like the mothers we have studied previously, the Witch of Endor shows herself to be a person of wisdom and understanding. She seems to intuit the danger in Saul's request, but she nonetheless complies with his demand. In answering his need, she brings the king of the newly established, but floundering nation, the encouragement he seeks. Though Saul is not successful in his campaign to lead Israel, the medium acts as a national mother by helping a royal figure. In this way, she actively engages in the political arena. The Israelites are at a crossroads, awaiting competent leadership, and her care for Saul eases a period of chaos in a transitional time.

CONCLUSION

We have made a case for the existence of metaphorical mothers within the Bible.

Though the meaning of term is not self-evident, we tried to provide definitive perimeters for the concept. Metaphorical mothers are women who "mother" either a nation or the royal figure who leads the nation. They are not necessarily biological mothers. Their motherhood is symbolic.

Deborah, whom the Bible labels, "mother in Israel," is a paradigm for our study. As Judges 4 demonstrates, she judges, advises, and finally leads Israel into battle. In contrast, the ancient epic poem of Judges 5 does not describe Deborah as judge or prophet, but emphasizes her status as a mother, suggesting that a metaphorical mother can possess assigned leadership traits, and act in ways not usually expected of a woman in the androcentric world of the Bible. Though the other women who follow our discussion of Deborah may not act militarily, as Deborah did, they influence the direction of social, political and religious history through word and deed. Miriam leads her people on their wanderings and rejoices in their salvation and newly acquired freedom. Esther submits herself to a life within the court of a pagan king, and risks her welfare to save her people from certain annihilation by the ruthless despot Haman. Finally, Huldah, Rahab, and the Witch of Endor, provide necessary hospitality and wisdom during momentous points in Israel's history. All of these women have in common that their lives powerfully influence the public sector. They mother their people metaphorically on a communal, and even national level.

NOTES

1. The term "mother in Israel" occurs elsewhere, but is not used as a title, as it is here in Judges. 2 Samuel 20:16–19 mentions a "city and mother in Israel," and is part of the speech of the wise woman of Abel.

2. Even though Miriam precede Deborah in the biblical record, we start with Deborah because she provides us with the model of the national mother.

3. Mieke Bal, *Death and Dissymmetry: The Politics of Coherence in the Book of Judges* (Chicago, Illinois: University of Chicago Press, 1988), 209. Deborah is first called "*eshet lapidot*." It is unclear whether this phrase indicates that she was the "wife of a man named Lapidot" or is describing her as a "woman of flames." The term fits her without any need to connect her to a husband. The problem of whether *eset* means "wife" is not unique to Deborah; see Cheryl Exum, "Deborah," in *Harper's Bible Dictionary* (San Francisco, California: Harper & Row, 1985), 214.

4. See note 3 above.

5. P.A.H. de Boer, *Fatherhood and Motherhood in Israelite and Judean Piety* (Leiden: Brill, 1974), 32

6. T. Frymer-Kensky, "Deborah 2," in *Women in Scripture* (Grand Rapids: Eerdmans Publishing, 2000), 67.

7. I take the verb *qamti* to be an archaic form, and thus, "you arose," rather than "I arose."

8. For an alternate version of the song, see Daniel J. Harrington, "Pseudo-Philo" in *The Old Testament Pseudepigrapha*, Vol. 2 (New York: Doubleday, 1985), 345–8.

9. *Eliyahu Rab.* (9)10; see also *Galatians* 3:28.

10. Daniel J. Harrington and A.J. Saldarini, *Targum Jonathan of the Former Prophets: Introduction, Translation, and Notes*, (Wilmington, Delaware: Michael Glazier, 1987), 65, note 5.

11. Tikvah Frymer-Kensky, *Reading the Women of the Bible* (New York: Schocken Books: 2002), 49.

12. Frymer-Kensky, 51.

13. Although the Bible does not mention that Miriam had children, later Jewish tradition could not tolerate her single status and rabbinic sources give her Caleb as a husband and Hur as a son. L.Bronner, *From Eve to Esther* (Louisville, Westminster John Knox Press, 1994), 169.

14. Frymer-Kensky, 28.

15. Athalya Brenner, *The Israelite Woman* (Sheffield: JSOT, 1985), 61.

16. Carey A. Moore, *Studies in the Book of Esther* (New York: Ktav Publishing House, 1982); *Esther: A New Translation with Introduction and Commentary* (New York: Doubleday, 1971); Michael Fox, *Character and Ideology in the Book of Esther* (Columbia: University of South Carolina, 1991); Kenneth Craig, *Reading Esther: A Case for the Literary Carnivalesque* (Louisville: John Knox Press, 1995).

17. S. Goldman, "Esther," in *The Five Megilloth: Hebrew Text, English Translation,* ed. A. Cohen (London, England: Soncino Press, 1946), 241; Lewis B. Paton, *A Critical and Exegetical Commentary on the Book of Esther* (Edinburgh, Scotland: T&T Clark, 1976), 300–302.

18. Claudia V. Camp, *Wisdom and the Feminine in the Book of Proverbs* (Sheffield, England: Almond Press, 1985), 140 ff.

19. *b. Megillah* 7a. The biblical book makes reference to a similar letter sent to all the Jews, in *Esther* 9:29f. Citing Esther 9:28, Maimonides states (*Mishneh Torah, Hilhot Megillah* 2, at the end) that while the words of the prophets and hagiographa would become void in the days of the Messiah, the scroll of Esther and holiday of Purim would continue forever. In Jewish tradition Haman is considered to be an Amalekite.

20. *b. Megillah* 7a.

21. There are minor differences in language between these two accounts, but for the most part, they are similar.

22. The meaning of Josiah's mother's name is relevant to our study. Her name, Jedidah (Heb.*yedida*), means "beloved of God." Perhaps we can infer from her name that she was a godly individual. Notably, King Solomon is also called Jedidiah, to acknowledge the close relationship he had with God.

23. Bronner, *From Eve to Esther* (Louisville: John Knox Press, 1994), 174–180; E. Deen, *All the Women of the Bible* (New York: Harper and Brothers Publishers, 1955), 145.

24. b.Meg. 14:29

25. I am indebted to T. Frymer-Kensky for noting the connection between Huldah and later biblical interpretation (*Reading the Women of the Bible*, 326).

26. One sanitizing version offered by some commentators is that she was an innkeeper. The root of the word *zonah*, (*zn*) is shared with the word *zon*, "to nourish," and is the key to transforming her into an innkeeper. Another sage suggests that she kept the perfumery. Josephus also depicts her as an innkeeper. For more information on Rahab, see my book, *From Eve to Esther*, p. 160.

27. The New Testament regards Rahab favorably in connection with her great faith. She is in the genealogy of Christ, but also as a person of great faith (Hebrews 11:31; James 2:25).

28. Thomas Overholt, "Medium of Endor," in *Women in Scripture*, 259.

29. Josephus, *Antiquities of the Jews* VI, 14.3–4.

Chapter Six

Unconventional Mothers

... the divine beings slept with the daughters of men, who bore them off-spring ...

Genesis 6:4b

Come, let us make our father drink wine, and let us lie with him, that we may maintain life through our father.

Genesis 30:19

Come into your brother's wife, perform the levirate act, and raise up seed for your brother.

Genesis 38:8

Children are the anchors that hold a mother to life.

Sophocles, *Phaedra*. Frag.619.

In this section we discuss women who become mothers via unconventional means and whose progeny are exceptional in some way. The first women we discuss produce the mythic Nephilim, the second women bring forth the ancestors of the Moabites and Ammonites, and the third woman gives birth to a forerunner of Israelite royalty. The stories we encounter in this chapter are of an etiological nature. They address the origins and beginnings of individuals and groups.

We do not read of the following mothers' interaction with their offspring, only of how they come into motherhood. How do these women feel about their children? How do these women raise their young? Unlike most of the other accounts of mothers in the Bible, these stories do not give us insight into a woman's behavior as mother. We only know that these women give birth through unorthodox means and in unusual circumstances. In some cases, they go to great lengths to conceive, using deceit and trickery to achieve their ends. Their children go on in biblical tradition to become noted personalities.

We mention these mothers because their examples give us a more complete portrait of the mother of the biblical world. We first discuss the mothers of Genesis 6 who mate with the "sons of God." We also look at Lot's daughters, who become mothers through incestuous means. We then analyze Tamar, Judah's daughter-in-law, who resorts to incest (according to Leviticus 18:15 a father-in-law is prohibited from having sexual relations with his daughter-in-law) in order to conceive and carry on the family line. Although these women become mothers through unorthodox methods, biblical tradition does not look upon them unfavorably. The laconic Hebrew text rarely offers value judgments, and it is no different in these morally troubling narratives. We merely read of the interactions of the characters and the end results of their decisions.

MOTHERS OF HEROES, OR MOTHERS OF WICKED BEINGS?

Genesis 6 records an unusual tale. Many biblical scholars have grappled with the account of the "divine beings" having sexual relations with "daughters of men:"

> Men began to increase upon the face of the earth and gave birth to daughters. The divine beings saw that the daughters of men were beautiful and they took wives for themselves from any they selected. And God said, "My spirit will not dwell in man forever, for he is flesh, but his days will be a hundred and twenty years. The Nephilim were on the earth in those days and also afterwards, when the divine beings came to the daughters of men, and they bore children. These were the mighty men of old, men of renown.
>
> Genesis 6:1–4

The story presents many questions. Who are the " divine beings ?" Does God limit human life span because of the rebellious actions of these divine creatures? Why are humans punished for the sins of immortal beings? Are the Nephilim of verse 4 connected with the offspring of the union between divine beings and humans of verse 2? Should we view the Nephilim positively or negatively?[1]

The description here of conception between the divine beings and daughters of men is highly unusual. Nowhere else does the Bible record such a union. Why do the biblical sources include this tale in the pre-antediluvian material of Genesis? If we view the brief legend in the context of the story of human history that was being developed in early Genesis, the account helps explain the wickedness that was prevalent upon the earth before God destroyed humanity through the great Flood. The mating between mortals and immortals, two unequal parties, disturbs the cosmic balance established in the creation order and angers God.

But what does this brief story tell us about motherhood? The daughters of men willingly consort with divine beings in order to achieve greater life spans for their offspring. Were they also hoping that their sons and daughters born through this unconventional union would gain immortality? This suggestion is plausible in light of the Tower of Babel account that follows later. The quest for human betterment, at the cost of antagonizing God, seems to be a major theme in Genesis 1–11. The mothers of Genesis 6 want their children to be strong and powerful, superhuman. We see these women as influential in that their behavior (along with the sons of God) has lasting impact on the human race. When they readily engage in sexual relations with the immortal creatures they allow the birth of a unique brand of beings, whose constitution was offensive to God, and whose existence prompted a divine decree of a shorter life span. The antediluvians lived to extraordinary ages; after this displeasing union of mortals and immortals, humans were granted as punishment only a hundred and twenty years according to the myth.

In our discussion on the mothers of the Nephilim (or *giborim*, "mighty men"?), we have asked many questions, but because of the laconic and mystical nature of the text, have provided few answers. Although we tried to translate and explain the event to bring clarity to a complex and enigmatic text, queries still remain. We include the study of the Genesis 6 passage because we believe it sheds light on the topic of motherhood. These women became unconventional mothers in the interest of strengthening the human race.

THE ENIGMA OF LOT'S DAUGHTERS

According to the Bible, Sodom is a vicious and violent society devoid of morality and ethics (Is.5:7; Ezek.16:49–50). The sin is of a social nature and the text never mentions any repentance undertaken by the people of Sodom and Gemorrah. On the contrary they are insubordinate and rebellious, and thus their behavior brings about the city's devastation. God sends destroying angels to wreak havoc on the townspeople and the whole city perishes (Gen. 19:13).

The story of Lot's daughters is disturbing and complicated. Angels visit Lot in Sodom to warn him of impending destruction. Townspeople, hearing that Lot has guests, surround Lot's house and demand that he surrender his visitors to their cruel pleasures. Lot offers instead his daughters to satisfy their sexual lust. The angels intervene and save the young women by striking the mob with blindness and rescuing Lot's daughters. Ultimately, Sodom is destroyed, as the angels had foretold. One of the most troubling matters of this story is Lot's willingness to surrender his virgin daughters to an unruly mob bent on rapine.[2]

This unsavory episode involving a father and his daughters leads us to comment on Lot's highly objectionable conduct. Rather than guarding his daughters and protecting their honor, he willingly gives them over to be raped by a mob. According to most biblical historians, Lot's behavior can be understood in light of ancient near eastern hospitality conventions.[3] Entrapped by these social standards, he offers his daughters rather than gives over his valued guests. Surprisingly, many modern commentators do not pass judgment on Lot's egregious behavior, but rather explain his actions by referring to these unusual hospitality conventions. However, Speiser picks up on character defects in Lot. Speiser writes, "he is undecided, flustered, ineffectual . . . he hesitates to turn his back on his possessions, and has to be led to safety by the hand. . . . Lot's irresoluteness makes him incoherent."[4] Like Speiser, rabbinic tradition which we will discuss below also finds fault with Lot. In the end, Lot is saved, not by his own merit, but ultimately because of God's mercy and his association with Abraham (Gen.19:16–18). The trajectory of the story of Lot shows a man who strays from his noble beginnings to lead a corrupt existence in Sodom.

Lot's name may be explained as stemming from the root, *m-l-t*, meaning, "to slip away." Conversely, his name also may come from the root *l-w-t*, meaning, "to be enclosed." Both roots speak to Lot's experience. He is "enveloped" in the wickedness of Sodom, and he also manages to escape the city, to "slip away" in the nick of time.

After our initial introduction to Lot's daughters in the mob story, we also encounter the women when they initiate incestuous intercourse with their father. This story is most significant to our discussion of motherhood. The biblical text reads:

> And the older one said to the younger, "Our father is old, and there is not a man on earth to consort with us in the way of the world. Come, let us make our father drink wine, and let us lie with him, that we may maintain life through our father." That night they made their father drink wine, and the older one went in and lay with her father; he did not know when she lay down or when she rose. The next day the older one said to the younger, "See, I lay with Father last night; let us make him drink wine tonight also, and you go and lie with him, that we may maintain life through our father." That night also they made their father

drink wine, and the younger one went and lay with him; he did not know when she lay down or when she rose. Thus the two daughters of Lot came to be with child by their father. The older one bore a son and named him Moab; he is the father of the Moabites today. And the younger also bore a son, and she called him Ben-ammi; he is the father of the Ammonites of today.

Genesis 19:30–38

In the belief that they and their father are the sole human survivors after Sodom's destruction, Lot's daughters seduce their father in order to produce further generations. The desire to become pregnant and repopulate the earth governs their decision to deceive their father. They give him wine, get him drunk, and take advantage of him in his intoxicated state. According to the text, they are successful in their pursuits. They both become pregnant by their father. What does this story of incest and violation tell us about motherhood? Does this literary account offer motherhood as a motive for licentious behavior? Or is it a story of remarkable courage to achieve the greater end of saving humanity?

This unusual account of the incestuous relationship between father and daughters gives expression to a woman's voice. The ubiquitous narrator gives a window into an ancient woman's thought life. When we read the text, we hear the aims and desires of Lot's older daughter. She is the mastermind behind the plan for progeny. Her tone is neither apologetic nor regretful, but confident and certain. She believes her course of action to be right and in the best interests of herself and her people. In the ancient world, having children for both men and women was the route by which one's future welfare was secured.[5] Thus, Lot's daughter was following an innate preservation instinct.

According to Frymer-Kensky, Lot's older daughter's actions remind us of those of her later descendent, Ruth the Moabite.[6] Both women are faced with the dilemma of how to conceive when neither has a husband. "When the posterity of their house is in peril, these women act unconventionally, even contra-conventionally, to preserve it."[7] Ruth, with Naomi's encouragement, aggressively pursues Boaz in order to secure future progeny, and her foremother, Lot's daughter, eagerly pursues an unconventional pregnancy in order to further the family line. Both women are concerned with perseverance of the clan, a common concern among other biblical mothers, and each woman goes to great lengths to further her aim.

Interestingly, the male patriarchal figure, Lot, in the story does not play the leading role, but rather is a passive actor in the pursuit of progeny. But though the biblical text indicates that Lot was not aware of any sexual molestation, some rabbis have suggested that he was conscious of the younger daughter's violation.[8] The rabbis say that the first time his elder daughter misled him, made him drunk, and seduced him, he was innocent by reason of his intoxication. The second time, however, he should have known better and resisted the seduction. The rabbinic commentary *Genesis Rabba* states:

> Come, let us make our father drink wine... that we may preserve seed of our father . . . and they made their father drink wine and he knew not when she lay down, and when she arose—*u-vekumah* ['and when she arose']: This word [*u-vekumah*] is dotted, intimating that he did not indeed know of her laying down, but he did know of her arising. . . . We would not know whether Lot lusted after his daughters, or they lusted after him, but that it says, *he that seperateth himself seeketh desire* (Prov 18:1), whence it follows that Lot desired his daughters.[9]

The rabbis base their explanation on the fact that the word *u-vequmah* ("when she got up") is written with certain diacritical marks (it is "dotted," as the Midrash says) above it in the verse (Gen. 19:33) "and he knew not when she lay down, and when she got up." The Sages say that the diacritical marks mean that although Lot did not know of her lying down, he did indeed know of her arising.[10] The dots above the text betray the underlying, genuine feelings and intentions of biblical characters. The rabbis thus hold him culpable for failing to resist the second seduction and for his willing participation. Not only do the Sages apply more lenient standards in judging the daughters, they in fact praise the two women as the progenitors of two nations.[11] They maintain that God tolerated the behavior of the elder daughter even though she brazenly proclaimed her son as being "from my father," (which was the meaning of the name "Moab" that she gave the child). The younger daughter is more modest, naming her child, Ben-ammi, "son of my people." Both daughters, however, are viewed favorably, while their father is seen as delinquent and indifferent in offering them protection, and passive in allowing their incestuous violation.

Since both the story of the violent mob of Sodom and the story of the rape of Lot by his daughters follow one another in the biblical text, are they literarily related? Did the biblical editor purposely place them side-by-side? Some commentators find purpose in the chronological ordering of the two accounts. The account of Lot giving over his virgin daughters stands in stark contrast to the account of his daughters' attempts to conceive. One story takes place in the city, the other in the hills. One story involves violation by an angry and foreign mob; the other involves violation by one's own family members. But perhaps the most significant contrast between the stories that relates to our topic of motherhood is the action taken by the angels recounted in the first tale. Before Lot's daughters could be violated, angels arrive on the scene to rescue them. No such rescuer comes to Lot's aid when he is violated. Does this suggest that the biblical narrators understood and approved of a woman's quest to conceive? We suggest that the objective and non-judgmental tone of the account of Lot's daughters demonstrates how important progeny is in the biblical mindset. Even incestuous rape is justifiable, if it continues the family line. That the biblical narrator portrays the women of the story assertively pursuing motherhood and proactively taking a role in their future and the future of the their people shows an awareness of maternal power on the part of the biblical text.

TAMAR—A WOMAN'S VINDICATION

We now want to discuss Tamar, who similar to Lot's daughters, resorts to desperate means to conceive a child. She is another unconventional mother. She uses the ruse of prostitution in order to attain her rightful status in society. According to the biblical account Tamar is married successively to two sons of Judah, both of whom die leaving her childless. Consistent with levirate law, she is entitled marriage by her husbands' brother, Judah's youngest son, to continue the family line. Judah sends Tamar home to wait for Shelah, his third son, to grow up. As time passes it becomes evident to Tamar that Judah has no intention of marrying her to his third son, and that she is doomed to the ignominy of childless widowhood.

The biblical text that relates the story of Tamar and her failed marriages reads as follows:

> Er, Judah's eldest son, was evil in God's eyes and God killed him. Judah said to Onan: "Come into your brother's wife, perform the levirate act, and raise up seed for your brother." Onan knew that the seed would not be for him and it happened that as he came to his brother's wife, he ejaculated on the earth without giving seed for his brother. What he did was evil in God's eyes, and he killed him too. Judah said to Tamar his daughter-in-law, "Sit as a widow in your father's house until Shelah my son grows up." . . . Tamar went and sat in her father's house.
> Genesis 38:7–11

Throughout the book we have noted the importance of names, both linguistically and literarily, in the Hebrew Bible and here we want to comment on the names in this story. Each of Judah's sons has names that could have foretold great things, but instead each one's life ends in disgrace. Er, who name is from the root, *'-w-r*, meaning "energetic" turns out to "barren," from the root, *'-r-r*. Onan, *'-w-n*, the root of whose name has dual connotation, variously meaning "vigor," or its opposite, "weariness," comes to "nothingness," a play on one of the root meanings. And ironically, Shelah, *shela*, which means "hers," is never rightfully given in marriage to Tamar. Shelah never becomes "hers" [Tamar's], because Judah is afraid that he too will die, as did his brothers. All the men in her life fail her and their names bespeak their character.

Tamar is trapped in the customs of biblical society. She is neither an independent widow, nor a dependent wife. She is an abandoned woman who is childless and betrayed by her father-in-law, so she devises a plan that, at the risk of her life, will enable her to bear a child, the only means for her to attain status in society and security in life.

The text records her deception:

> ... She took off her widow's garb, covered her face with a veil, and wrapping herself up, sat down at the entrance to Eanim, which is on the road to Timnah, for she saw that Shelah was grown up, yet she had not been given to him as wife. When Judah saw her, he took her for a harlot; for she had covered her face. So he turned aside to her by the road. . . . "What pledge shall I give you?" She replied, "Your seal and cord, and the staff from which you carry."
>
> Genesis 38:14–18

Tamar takes matters into her own hands, and pretends to be a harlot in order to conceive. The biblical text is puzzling on this point, reporting that "she covered her face with a veil." The account goes on later to add that when Judah sees her, he believes her to be a harlot, for "she had covered her face" (Gen 38:15).[12] She then waits for her father-in-law, who does not recognize her and solicits her for a sexual act. They agree on a price (a kid from his flock), and Tamar carefully obtains from him a surety in advance, asking for items that will serve as identification: his signet, cord, and staff. They conclude their agreed transaction, and Tamar thus conceives a child. Afterward she resumes her widows' garb. When Judah later sends the kid in payment for his act, he is told that there is no harlot in that place. Three months later he is informed that his daughter-in-law had "played the harlot . . . [and was] with child by harlotry." Judah calls for her to be brought forward to be burnt, whereupon Tamar shows the three items and says to him "I am with child by the man to whom these belong." Judah acknowledges them as his own, and declares that Tamar was more righteous than himself, because he had withheld his son from her. In the construction of the story (which we acknowledge was framed within an androcentric worldview), a male character (Judah) recognizes the importance and value of motherhood and future progeny. Judah's support of Tamar lends legitimacy to her cause and under girds her maternal instinct.

Though many women of biblical world found themselves in the unfortunate position of being widowed and childless, few had the courage to take matters into their own hands as Tamar did. This indicates that Tamar, in keeping with her name, which means "date tree," was strong and sturdy. The date tree was also symbol of fertility, an irony, given her barrenness in two marriages.[13] Tamar actively takes steps to change her destiny, by an act that defies the patriarchal order, in the interest of allowing her, ultimately, to fulfill herself according to its terms.

Although Tamar was a widow, her childlessness meant that she did not possess the independence of the widow with children. A widow with children could feel the security of knowing she would be looked after, because her children would inherit their father's estate, and could be assumed to provide for their mother. A childless widow, in contrast, received no estate. Under the laws of levirate marriage, the childless widow was at the mercy of the brother-in-law who was supposed to marry her, but who might refuse, leaving her in an untenable and insecure position. Widows were not as desirable for marriage as virgins. Tamar took a great risk in her bold solution to her predicament, as she was regarded in society as a married woman and therefore subject to the death penalty for adultery.

A wife did not inherit from her husband, and Tamar acts according to a logic dictated by this patriarchal fact. The patriarchal laws of marriage and inheritance make it more urgent for her to acquire a child than to find a husband, and this she shrewdly contrives to accomplish. She recognizes that only motherhood would save her from a state of oblivion and further, grant her status and power in the social world of the Bible.

Deception is a key feature in the Tamar narrative, but is not unique to her story. In fact, women figure prominently in several narratives turning on the use of deception: Sarah's brother-sister ruse staves off the death of Abraham at the hands of King Abimelech (Gen 20:1–18); Rebecca sends off Jacob to his father all decked out as Esau (Gen 27:8–16); Rachel deceives her father by hiding the household gods (Gen 31:34); the midwives in Egypt fail to kill the Israelite newborns (Exod 1:15–21); Michal the daughter of Saul deceives her father and helps David escape (I Sam 19:11–17); Jael kills Sisera by deception, as she welcomes him to her tent (Judges 4:17–24).

Some scholars have suggested that women, being the weaker party, have often resorted to deception to oppose the stronger party;[14] however, men too used these sorts of ploys to their advantage, even on occasions when they are not the weaker party, as in the stories of Ehud and the King of Moab (Judg 3:12–31); Joshua and the Gibeonites (Josh 9:3–16); Jacob and Laban and so on. Judah, along with his brothers, tricks his father into thinking Joseph had been killed by wild beasts (Gen.37:31–34). Women, however, are not only noted for their frequent recourse to deceptive stratagems, they are characterized as frivolous and indecisive when they resort to ruse, whereas when men use these methods, they are credited with political astuteness and presence of mind.[15] Susan Niditch states:

> "One of the biblical authors' favorite narrative patterns is that of the trickster. Israelites tend to portray their ancestors and thereby imagine themselves as underdogs, as people outside the establishment who achieve success in roundabout, irregular ways. One of the ways marginals confront those in power and achieve their goals is through deception or trickery. The improvement in their

status may be only temporary, for to be a trickster is to be of unstable status, to be involved in transformation and change."[16]

Awareness of this issue of deception has come to light as a result of modern, feminist scholarship. Instead of viewing deception and trickery as a negative thing, scholars have come to view deceit and manipulation as a positive way (sometimes the only way) in which a marginal character can achieve success or bring about his or her aims. Tamar uses a ruse to accomplish her goal of conception, and finds success in her manipulation.

CONCLUSION

In this chapter we discussed unconventional mothers. All of the women from the stories above find their maternal longing fulfilled through unorthodox means. We first discussed the "daughters of men" who gave birth (apparently) to the mythic Nephilim. We then relayed the stories of Lot's daughters who violated their father in order birth and perpetuate the human race. We also looked at Tamar, who through skillful ploy, conceived by her father-in-law.

The above women resort to highly unusual methods to become pregnant, yet the biblical text records the stories and does not pass judgment on their behavior. Is this because the biblical narrators viewed perpetuity of the clan as all-important? So much so, that any transgression committed in order to continue the family line was justifiable? We see these women as both admirable and courageous, as they are willing to risk their reputations for the sake of continuing the family line.

NOTES

1. The topic of Nephilim is an interesting one. Besides here, the term occurs only in Numbers 13:33, where they are also called the "sons of Anak." Later interpretative tradition attempt to explain who the Nephillim are. The Apocrypha and Pseudepigrapha refer to the Nephilim, usually with reference to their pride and wickedness, and to God's judgment upon them (Baruch 3:26–28).

2. Rabbinic tradition indicts Lot, but excuses the later behavior of his daughters, see my discussion in *From Eve to Esther*, 113–147.

3. G.von Rad, *Genesis: A Commentary*, (London: SCM Press, 1972), 218. As an aside, we mention Judges 19, the story in which the daughter (the concubine) is given to the mob who surrounds the house. In that account the woman is brutalized and killed, not saved by angels as were Lot's daughters.

4. E. A. Speiser, *Genesis* (New York: Doubleday & Company, 1964) p. 143.

5. Ken Stone, "Daughters of Lot," in *Women in Scripture* ed. by C. Meyers (Grand Rapids: Eerdmans Publishing, 2000), 179.

6. Ruth is discussed at length and from a different angle in Chapter 4.

7. Frymer-Kensky, 263.

8. Ibid.

9. *Gen R* 51:8–10.

10. *Gen R* 51:8.

11. Modern scholars offer different explanations for the origins of the Moabite and Ammonite peoples, see John Skinner, ed., *The International Critical Commentary: Critical and Exegetical Commentary on Genesis* (Edinburgh: T. & T. Clark, 1969), p. 314.

12. Puzzling, in that covering oneself is usually considered proper, modest behavior, not shameless and loose. But perhaps the description was necessary to explain how Judah could find her impossible to recognize.

13. Ps. 92:12; Mordecai A. Friedman, "Tamar, A Symbol of Life: The Killer Wife Superstition in the Bible and Jewish Tradition," *AJS Review* 15 (1990), 23–26.

14. Robert C. Culley, "Structural Analysis: is it Done with Mirrors?" *Interpretation* 28 (1974), 174–181.

15. Fuchs cogently makes this point in her article, "'For I Have the Way of Women': Deception, Gender, and Ideology in Biblical Narrative," *Semeia 42* (1988), 68–83.

16. Susan Niditch, "Genesis," in *The Women's Bible Commentary* edited by Carol Newsom and Sharon Ringe (Louisville, Westminster/John Knox Press, 1992), 18.

Chapter Seven

The Motherly Role of God

As a mother comforts her son so I will comfort you.

Isaiah 66:13

A mother is a mother still, the holiest thing alive.

S.T. COLERIDGE, *The Three Graves. St.10*

The Bible portrays the many-sided activities of God who is concerned with human life and experience. Indeed the role of the mother is so important that the Bible sees fit to describe God as a mother performing her duties to family and society. Significantly, when given feminine traits, God is never cast in the role of wife, daughter or sister; rather, God is cast as Mother, further highlighting the special status accorded to motherhood. While the patriarchal character of Scripture has been well documented,[1] until recently few scholars noted the range of maternal imagery that is used in association with God.[2] This is well illustrated by the absence of articles on the word "mother" in most Bible dictionaries. Instead, the mother is subsumed under the topic of "family," as if the topic does not merit a separate article. The first volume of the translation of Botterweck and Ringgren's *Theological Dictionary of the Old Testament*, for example, appeared in 1974, when feminism was aflame in the United States, and yet does not have a single entry under *'em*, "mother," but a highly comprehensive one exists for "father"! Even today, one encounters an unfortunate dearth of academic resources on the topic of "mother," when typing the word in to a search engine on the Internet! Nevertheless, the discipline of women's studies has influenced scholars to take up this theme, some of whom have addressed the difficulty of attributing women's roles to God.[3] We include this chapter on the motherly role of God in the Bible to underscore the importance of the mother figure in ancient Israel and to show that a mother's duties were held in high esteem—as even God is imagined as performing these female functions.

It should be mentioned that some scholars link such maternal images to the mother goddess figures in Near Eastern mythology, especially the influence of the cult of Asherah.[4] But we do not delve into the complex study of goddesses, as our focus is on showing the biological female functions attributed to God. Rather than looking to a possible influence of Akkadian or Canaanite goddess worship on Israelite belief and practice, we show how the view of the human mother in ancient Hebrew society is reflected in the biblical imagery on God. The complex feminine imagery describes God's relationship to the people of Israel. Interestingly, whenever a feminine role is attributed to God, it is always presented in the role of a *mother*. Of particular concern are maternal imagery occurring in the Pentateuch, Hosea, Jeremiah, and Isaiah. The most striking feminine images compare God's actions to those of a mother bearing, caring for, carrying, and comforting her children. Our study also elaborates on key verbs: *harah* (to impregnate), *yatzar* (to form), *henik* (to nurse), *yalad*, (to give birth), and others that always used to describe God's mothering.

The story of the Exodus, narrated in several books of the Bible, is particularly informative in our discussion of the maternal relationship between God and the people of Israel. In this account God is depicted as reacting to the people's murmuring by supplying them with food and water, a role traditionally played by women. For instance, the biblical type scenes at a well always depict the woman as drawing water to supply the needs of the family.[5] When the children of Israel complain about the food provided for them, Moses tellingly uses feminine imagery to record their protest:

> Did I conceive this people, did I bring them forth?
> That thou should say to me, carry them in your bosom
> as a nurse that carries the suckling child,
> to the land that thou didst swear to give to their fathers.[6]
>
> Num. 11:12

The picture of God as fulfilling the functions of a mother is clearly implied in this passage. The root *harah* conjures up the image of pregnancy. The root *yalad* is used for bringing forth children. Moses complains about the unbearable burden that the people are to him. He protests that, after all, he is neither the mother nor the nurse of the people, and is therefore not obligated to fulfill maternal duties towards them. Moses' reproach of God intimates that God, in fact, is the mother of the people. This charge is evidenced by the repeated stress on the pronoun "I," suggesting: "not I, but you." The relevance of this reproach is that God's care is compared to that of a mother's. We are left with a cogent picture of God's performing the functions of mother. God, not Moses, cares most effectively and significantly, as a Mother-figure, for God's Israelite children.

Deuteronomy 32:18 supports a similar idea:

> You were unmindful of the Rock that begot you/
> Forgot the God who brought you forth.

The word in the first line of the parallel phrase translated "begot" comes from a verb root *yalad* which is usually used in relation to a woman giving birth, bearing or bringing forth a child. The verb translated "who brought you forth" in the second line is a participle verb formed from the Hebrew root *holel*, which describes a woman giving birth with pain. The verb offers an image of God who brought forth Israel with difficulty, and formed them into a nation. Even though the verbs are conjugated in the masculine the whole image is one that is altogether maternal.

The following verses in Deuteronomy 32 present another motherly image:

> Like an eagle who rouses his nest
> That flutters over the young
> spreading out its wings, catching them,
> bearing them on its pinions . . .
> the LORD alone did lead him
>
> Deut. 32:11 ff

Using the image of a family of birds, the Deuteronomist expresses God's mothering role toward Israel. Though all the verbs are again conjugated in the masculine the illustration, too, is strictly feminine. The gendered language reminds one of the tendencies today to continue to speak of "mankind," when referring to both women and men. We draw attention to this verse because it poignantly conveys God's maternal traits.

In Hosea, God is described as the parent who teaches the son to walk, heals his wounds and feeds the hungry infant. These activities traditionally belong to the mother, not to the father. Though for the most part, the Bible rejects depicting God as a human, Hosea offers a paradox of both affirming and denying anthropomorphic language in this passage. The opposition is between God and human beings, the latter being vengeful, the former merciful. So Hosea 4:4 does not stress the masculine, but the *human* personality. This concept is dramatically conveyed by Hosea 11:1–11, which states emphatically: "For I am God *(El)* and not a male *('ish)*." In other words, God in Hosea is not limited by his gender (as a man). Rather, God is regarded as possessing both feminine and masculine attributes, both the nature and function of mother and father. God is simultaneously both sexes and both parents. The limitations of language often prevent this fuller implication from being concretely conveyed, but nonetheless, God's male and female traits emerge upon closer analysis.

Phyllis Trible argues that God plays a feminine role when he makes clothes for his people.[7] In Genesis, God makes clothes for Adam and Eve and the verb *'asah* is used here as elsewhere (Gen. 3:21; Prov. 31:21 ff). The verb *'asah* occurs 2622 times in the Hebrew Bible and is thus a very general, all-purpose verb. When applied to God *'asah* can have a variety of meanings. In Exilic Isaiah 65:17, 66:22 and Genesis 1:7, 16 it is used with the verbs *yasar* and *bar'a* to describe God's creative activities. The image is repeated later in biblical literature. "Forty years you sustained them in the wilderness so that they lacked nothing; their clothes did not wear out, their feet did not swell" (Nehemiah 9:21). Here the verb is not *'asah* but *lo balu* ("did not wear out"). We conclude from the language in Nehemiah 9:21 that not only is God a seamstress but the clothes God sews endure. Nehemiah does not speak about making clothes, but rather about preserving them. The making of clothes suggests a divine miracle rather than human activity.[8] Moreover, Nehemiah's description does not represent ordinary tailoring but rather puts forth a particular theology. Still the image has nonetheless a maternal connotation, since mothers provide the clothing for the family. Similarly, God as a divine parent, God makes sure his people are properly attired.

God cares for his people as a mother, but perhaps more significantly, the Bible also alludes to God's giving birth to his people. The image of birthing attracted the attention of many writers and prophets in the Bible. Strangely, however, the positive aspect of giving birth, the creation of new life, was never stressed as much as the accompanying pain and suffering. Birth imagery appears most frequently and ironically in the book of the bachelor prophet Jeremiah.[9] He describes labor as a frightening ordeal and uses it as a metaphor for a moment when a warrior wanes weak. Jeremiah states in his doom oracle:

Thus said the LORD, we have heard a cry of panic, of terror, no peace

Ask now and see can a man bear a child?
Why then do I see every man with his hands on his loins
like a woman in labor? Why has every face turned pale?
Alas! that day is so great, there is none like it;
it is a time of distress for Jacob.

Jeremiah 30:5–7

Giving birth appears mostly as a negative experience, a labor that turns warriors into women, and exposes them as vulnerable, weak and cowardly. Often

Jeremiah speaks of giving birth figuratively to depict the anguish and agony that cripples the people when they hear the approaching enemy. "Anguish has overwhelmed us, pain like that of a woman in childbirth" (Jer. 6:24). The people are paralyzed by great fear. To Jeremiah, the image of a woman in travail powerfully expresses the terror and suffering of a people about to be sacked.

Unlike Jeremiah, exilic Isaiah[10] strikingly stresses the positive side of the birth experience. The pains and pangs of travail express unlimited pain and suffering, but more significantly show that new hope and life emerge from this experience. Isaiah depicts God as enduring the pains of childbirth.

> For a long time I have held my peace
> I have kept still and restrained myself:
> Now I will cry out like a woman in travail
> I will gasp and pant.
>
> Isaiah 42:14

The poet-prophet displays a galaxy of pictures from creation to redemption, from former things to latter things. The previous verse speaks about God as a warrior:

> The LORD goes forth like a mighty man,
> like a man of war he stirs up his fury
> He cries out, he shouts aloud,
> he shows himself mighty against his foes.
>
> Isaiah 42:13

The prophet uses the simile of a woman in travail to reinforce the break in God's silence and to show God's readiness to take action. The image of God enduring the pains of childbirth has a dual purpose: first to illustrate how terrifying God's shrieks are which alert the entire universe of God's changed intentions. Shaken by convulsive emotions, God groans, God gasps and pants like a woman about to give birth. These are divine shrieks that shake the world. Second the verse stresses another aspect of birth, namely its reviving quality. From the throes of these pains and pangs a new world would emerge. Birth is a creative concept. This verse is part of a salvation oracle, figuratively foretelling the birth pangs of redemption and a new creation. This image echoes the positive experience of birth in Genesis 4:1, where Eve joyously exclaims, "I have acquired a male child with God." Whereas Jeremiah depicts the negative side of birth and pregnancy, mirroring the punishment given in Genesis 3:16, "in pain shall you bear children," Isaiah portrays the positive potentials of birth.

God, laden with offspring, is an image often encountered in Exilic Isaiah:

> Harken to me, O House of Jacob, all the remnant of Israel who have been borne by me from the womb, carried from the womb, and until old age I am He, and to grey hairs am I carrying you. I will both bear, carry and save (46:3).

The participle "borne" and the expression "carried from the womb," all conjure up the image of God carrying and bearing a child. The verb *'amas* means to carry a load. Although it never depicts a woman with child, *'amas* effectively conjures up the image of pregnant woman. The verse indicates however that the divine bearer and carrier achieves more than the human mother, for he will not only bear, carry and deliver, but he will go on in perpetuity to perform miracles on Israel's behalf. God's mothering is eternal.

Particularly telling in this context is the verb *va'amallet*, translated, "I will rescue," from the root *m-l-t*, whose primary meaning is "to slip away," or "to deliver." It can mean "to escape," thus here, "to rescue." This meaning brings to mind the picture presented in Isaiah 66:7–9, where the word employed is *vehimlita*, "she cast out [a male child]."

> Before she was in labor she gave birth;
> Before her pain came upon her
> she cast out a male child.

The image in the verse is almost mysterious. A painless birth of an unidentified woman is described. Eventually her identity is disclosed. She is Zion.

> For as soon as Zion was in labor
> she brought forth her children.
>
> Isaiah 66:8

Zion's giving birth is a unique metaphor and meant as a miraculous and sudden birth indicative of the dawning of a new age. The LORD identifies with the event:

> Shall I bring to the birth and not cause to bring forth? says the LORD: shall I, who cause to bring forth, shut the womb? says your God.
>
> Isaiah 66:9

Exilic Isaiah describes God's love as stronger than even motherly love.

> Can a woman forget her suckling infant that she should have no compassion on the child of her womb? Even these may forget, yet I will not forget you.
>
> Isaiah 49:15

While Exilic Isaiah focuses on God as mother, the Book of Psalms describes God's love as fatherly love:

> As a father has compassion on his children
> so the LORD has compassion on those who fear him.
>
> Psalms 103:13

The Bible offers a picture and a precedent for both fatherly and motherly love. The image of the comforting mother, which will be discussed below, occurs once in Isaiah (66:13). The image of the comforting father occurs once in Psalms. Exilic Isaiah used the motherly image often, while the father's love features in later liturgies. The use of both fatherly and motherly images to express God's love shows a certain equanimity between the two parents.

Likewise, in midrashic homilies the Talmudic teachers allowed themselves considerable latitude in shedding light on the mystery of the deity by comparing God to human beings of both sexes. The following passage quoted in the name of Shemuel bar Nahman, is most striking:

> It is the wont of the father to have mercy,
> Like as the father has compassion upon his children
> so has the Lord compassion upon them that fear Him;
> and it is the wont of the mother to comfort,
> as one whom his mother comforts, so will I comfort you
> God said: 'I shall do as both father and mother.'[11]

I should point out that the *shekhinah*, with her feminine gender, comes close in Talmudic sources to being regarded as a feminine manifestation of the deity. A fourth century Palestinian teacher, Rabbi Aha, says:

> When she left the Sanctuary, she returned to caress and kiss its walls and columns, and cried and said: 'Be in peace, O my Sanctuary, be in peace, O my royal palace, be in peace, O my precious house, be in peace from now on, be in peace.[12]

The *shekhinah* as the feminine aspect of God is fully discussed in the Kabbalistic sources, a subject that is beyond the ambit of this book.

Isaiah states the deepest human love is that of a mother to her suckling child (*'ulah*), because the infant is completely dependent on the mother for its very survival (Isaiah 49:15). This verse in Exilic Isaiah suggests that God's love is deeper even than this human bond of love. The use of the image of mother was the most effective and powerful way to present God's compassion for his people. No other metaphor would suffice.

In spite of the above observations concerning the use of the mother image, the phrase about fatherly love features prominently in religious literature, and in later Jewish prayers, while the feminine picture of motherly love is ignored. The reason for this bias is related to the authors of the prayers being male and relating more to androcentric rather than gynomorphic imagery.

Trible discusses the physical and psychic meanings of *rehem*, "womb," as a most appropriate term to describe God's compassion.

> Designating a place of protection and care the womb (*rehem*) is a basic metaphor of divine compassion. The metaphor begins with a physical organ unique to the female and extends to psychic levels in the plural noun *rahamim*, mercies, in the adjectival form *rahum*, merciful, and in uses of the verb *ruham*, to show mercy. It moves from the literal to the figurative, from the concrete to the abstract.[13]

The word *rahum* is often combined with the word *hannun* in the Bible to describe God's nature as merciful and gracious.[14] It is possible that the word *hannun* is related to the noun *hen*, "grace," and originally meant, "to long for" in the sense of the maternal instinct. Though only used of God, *rahum* is not the language of the father who creates by begetting but of the mother who creates by nourishing in the womb.[15] In Jeremiah the verbal form *'arahem* occurs in a consolation oracle replete with feminine imagery (Jer. 30:15–22). In light of the suggested origin of the word *rahamim* from its associations with the root for womb one should translate *rahamim* as *motherly compassion*. Isaiah conveys the physical and psychic meanings of womb (Isaiah 49:15).[16] By juxtaposing God and mother, the prophet expresses the depth of transcendent love. The exilic prophet employs moving maternal imagery to suggest the unfathomable love of God for his suffering people. God is depicted as a comforting mother by Isaiah: "As one whom his mother comforts so will I comfort you" (Isaiah 66:13). Most commentaries on Isaiah either paraphrase the verse or fail to explain the gynomorphic imagery.

Targum Jonathan, an early translation of the Prophets, interprets: "As a man is comforted by his mother so My word will comfort you,"[17] and so avoids gynomorphic imagery. This is in keeping with his exegetical approach that eliminates anthropomorphisms. Rashi, the leading medieval commentator on the Bible and Talmud, does not refer to this unusual image, while another medieval commentator, RaDak (acronym for Rabbi David Kimchi, l1608–1235), explains it to mean that as one whom his mother comforted after he had experienced much suffering, so God will comfort Israel after the troubled exile experience. Another exegete, Mezudat David (who lived in the 18th century and whose real name was David Altschuler), comments that it is characteristic of the mother rather than the father to offer comfort and consolation.

More modern commentators either ignore or paraphrase the verse following the precedent set by the medieval exegetes. ShaDal (Samuel David Luzzatt [1800–1865]), claims that this verse unravels the mystery of the previous parable dealing with Zion as a woman suckling her child. God is the comforter and Jerusalem will be the place of comfort. Samuel Krauss' Hebrew commentary (1866–1948) follows Luzzatto. With the exception of Claus Westerman and A. S.Herbert, many commentaries ignore the gynomorphic aspect. In his recent commentary, Westermann makes a cogent comment:

> This is the first time in the Old Testament that the witness borne to YHWH breaks through the reserve which elsewhere it observes so strictly and associates feminine predications with him.[18]

Although Westermann's reference is interesting because it illustrates that more recent commentaries are beginning to take note of God's maternal aspect.

The exegetes of the Hebrew Bible, like the writers of world history were primarily male and they perceived the world as many still do in spite of the rise of feminism, through the exclusive lens of male experience. In another recent commentary Herbert takes the term "mother" as a reference to Zion and not to God.

> She (Zion) is described as the mother of the people of God and therefore the earthly counterpart of God, who in a remarkable phrase is also likened to a mother comforting her children.[19]

Biblical scholars' inability to cope with gynomorphic imagery is also illustrated by Jeremiah 51:5. Many commentators changed the reading of the text from 'alman to 'almanah, to prevent the possibility of seeing God as the widow and the people as the husband, a reversal of the usual imagery, in which God appears husband and Israel as wife. The commentators do not even note the problem, but only change the wording. In his commentary Laetsch gives the best translation. Although he does not indicate that the Hebrew text has 'alman, Laetsch translates the noun with an appropriate word, "widowed," rather than "forsaken." Exilic Isaiah depicts Zion on two occasions as a forsaken woman but employs the Hebrew word 'azuvah for depicting her lonely state and need for redemption by a redeemer.[20]

When the biblical narrators recall ancestors they usually refer to the patriarchs only. However, here the prophet strays from convention and calls the people to:

> Look unto the rock from whence you were hewn, and unto the hole of the pit whence you were dug Look unto Abraham your father, and unto Sarah that bore you.
>
> Isaiah 51:2

Sarah is mentioned along side Abraham as an important ancestor of the people. The matriarchs are not nearly as frequently mentioned as the patriarchs but there are a few instances where the matriarchs do feature. Jeremiah describes Rachel weeping for her children (Jer. 31:15-17), and Micah recalls that the prophetess Miriam together with her brothers Moses and Aaron redeem the people from the Egyptian exile (Micah 6:4).

In this chapter we have noted the various forms of feminine imagery in the Hebrew Bible referring to God in a maternal role. The most striking references are those that depict God's activities as a mother bearing, carrying, caring for and comforting children. A significant fact is that whereas Isaiah 1-39 employs few feminine images, Isaiah 40-66 draws imagery from family and female experience. A unifying feature of chapters 40-66 is the frequent appearance of feminine forms and the featuring of female experience. The foregoing survey of maternal imagery ascribed to God finds its depth and breadth in the words of Exilic Isaiah. The home and family is at the center of all this prophet's metaphors, similes and personifications. This institution of the home is the only stable feature of life left to the exiles. The father as husband, shepherd, and warrior appears but the focus now includes the mother and her care of the children.

Images of the father and mother, the suckling child, sons and daughters, bride and groom, marriage, divorce, barrenness, widowhood and their accompanying customs fill the prophetic pages in chapters 40-66 of Isaiah. The women's world is mirrored in these chapters by imagery of the bride, the mother, the nursing woman, the barren woman, the widow redeemed from her lonely state, and the fruitful mother embracing her sons and daughters. This illustrates the prophet's propensity to draw upon family and female imagery to articulate his message. He relies on one area of security left to an exiled people—the family—and in that sphere the woman's role is most significant.

Maternal images of God, as we have shown, appear throughout the Hebrew Bible. The mother is a person of influence, and the fact that God poses as a motherly figure demonstrates the power and importance of the mother in the home and beyond. Although most readers of the Bible often conceive of God as father, we hope to have shown that God's role as mother is equally important.

NOTES

1. Roland De Vaux, *Ancient Israel*, vol. 2 (New York: McGraw-Hill, 1965); Johs. Pederson, *Israel: Its Life and Culture*, vol. 2 (Denmark: Dyva & Jeppesen, 1965).

2. Phyllis Trible,*God and the Rhetoric of Sexuality* (Philadelphia: Fortress Press, 1978), 508–52.

3. See Phyllis Trible, "Depatriarchalising in Biblical Interpretation," *Journal of the American Academy of Religion* XI (1973): 283–303; Mayer Gruber, *The Motherhood of God and Other Studies* (Atlanta, Georgia: Scholars Press, 1992), 3–17.

4. Carol Meyers, "Female Images of God in the Hebrew Bible" in *Women in Scripture*, Meyers, ed. (Grand Rapids, Michigan: Houghton Mifflin, 2000), 526. See also Tikva Frymer-Kensky, *In the Wake of the Goddesses, Women, Culture, and the Biblical Transformation of Pagan Myth* (New York: Fawcett Columbine of Ballantine Books, 1992), 155–159.

5. The type scenes are narrative episodes connected with the careers of biblical heroes usually catching the protagonist at a critical or very important moment in life, i.e. biblical scenes of heroes and heroines meeting at the well. See: Robert Alter, *The Art of the Biblical Narrative* (Basic Books, Inc. 1980), 51 ff.

6. Johannes G. Botterweck, and Helmer Ringgren, *Theological Dictionary of the Old Testament*, vol. 1 (Eerdmans Publishing, 1972), 17.

7. Trible, *ibid.*

8. Other miraculous interventions that occur in the Pentateuch such as the falling of the manna and the supplying of water and meat could be examined to see whether they fall within the purview of our theme but I think not.

9. I speculate that Jeremiah is a bachelor because, unlike Hoseah, Isaiah, Ezekiel, and others, the book never mentions that the prophet had a wife or children. See Jer. 4:31; 6:24; 13:21; 22:23; 30:6; 48:41; 49:24; 50:43.

10. I refer to Is. 40–66 as Exilic Isaiah. Many modern scholars describe chapters 408–55 as Deutero-Isaiah and still others ascribe the last third of Isaiah (chapters 56–66) to Trito-Isaiah.

11. *Pesiqta Rab.* 139a. See also Raphael Patai, *The Hebrew Goddess* (Avon Books, 1978), 115.

12. *Lamentations Rab.* Proem, (brief introduction) 3rd edition (London: Soncino Press, 1983) xxv: 50–51.

13. Trible, op. cited.

14. See Psalms 114:4; Ps. 85:15; Joel 2:13; Jonah 4:2 etc.

15. Though the word clearly has maternal overtones, it is also used in reference to a father's love for his children, c.f.Psalm 103:13

16. Samuel Terrien, "Toward a Biblical Theology of Womanhood," *Religion in Life*, vol. 42, 1973: 322 ff.

17. *Mikraot Gedolot to the Later Prophets Isaiah and Jeremiah* (New York: Pardes Publishing House, 1957), 93.

18. Claus Westermann, *Isaiah 40–66* (Philadelphia, Pennsylvania: Westminster Press (SCM Press Ltd.), 1969), 420.

19. A. S. Herbert, *Isaiah 408–66*, Cambridge Bible Commentary (London, England and St. Louis, Missouri: Cambridge University Press, 1975), 194.

20. Theo Laetsch, *Jeremiah*, Bible Commentary (Concordia Publishing House, 1965) 359; cf. Isa. 54:6–7, 60:15–16, and 62:4 for Exilic Isaiah's use of the image of the forsaken woman redeemed by her *go'el*, her husband, referring to the well-known biblical custom in ancient Israel (Genesis 38; Deut. 25:1–4; book of Ruth).

Conclusion

I will bless her so that she will give rise to nations; rulers of peoples shall issue from her.

Genesis 17:16

There has been a basic contradiction throughout patriarchy: between the laws and sanctions designed to keep women essentially powerless, and the attribution to mothers of almost superhuman power (of control, of influence, of life-support).

ADRIENNE RICH
Motherhood: The Contemporary Emergency and the Quantum Leap[1]

I began this project with the premise that mothers in biblical tradition make concrete, identifiable, and positive contributions to their families and often influence their societies at large. I conclude this study reiterating that the influence of biblical mothers on their children is to be recognized, appreciated, and granted serious attention by students of the Bible. Although some scholars have argued that women of the Bible are powerless pawns living within the throes of patriarchy, I have contended in this work that the mother in the biblical world has unassigned power. Although she does not acquire a position through socially and culturally accepted means, she influences the destiny of her inner circle and the wider public.

Each chapter explores a different aspect of biblical motherhood through detailed analysis of various female figures. We initially looked at the first mothers of the Bible, the mothers and sons of Genesis, whose relationships reflect the social milieu of premonarchic Israel. The Genesis mothers are clan mothers, women who exercise their influence within a tribal setting. These mothers are looking to impact their families on a macro-level through directing the destiny of their sons on a micro-level. Although the mothers of Genesis at first glance have limited power, they find a voice through their sons whose actions they influence, and even at times manipulate to achieve their goals. The mothers of the early historical books are mothers of a budding nation. They are similar to the mothers of Genesis in that they yearn for children, especially sons, and then seek power through their sons. Unlike the matriarchs, these women are mothering in an age of transition, when a loose confederation of tribes is coalescing into a solidified nation. They also differ from their earlier counterparts in that they do not desperately yearn to give birth, but seem fulfilled by involving themselves in other arenas of social life. The chapter on wise women and queen mothers explores a new dimension of biblical motherhood. Wise women are the female sages of old who counseled king and commoner alike, employing their maternal wisdom. Queen mothers, as their name suggests, combine the preoccupations of a mother with those of a royal figure. They are privy to court machinations and their influence and counsel manages to affect, at times, a whole nation. These women, the wise women and queen mothers of the Bible, best represent the scope of the biblical mothers' influence, operating not only through a maternal attachment but also through their sense of worldly wisdom. In a way, these are political women who aspire to move outside the domestic realm and affect the larger public domain, namely the royal court. We then discussed biblical mothers and daughters, first delving into the use of the biblical metaphor and then discussing the few concrete examples peppered throughout Israel's literary record. Although the text records a small number of actual accounts, we included in our study the compelling relationship between Ruth and Naomi and the mentoring, safe, loving relationship between the Shulamite and her mother in *Song of Songs*. The next chapter postulated a new category of mother, namely that of Metaphorical Mother. This chapter examined some of the most dynamic and memorable female figures of the Hebrew Bible, namely Deborah, Miriam and Esther, and lesser-known mothers, Hulda, Rahab, and the Necromancer of Endor. These metaphorical mothers wield influence on the state level, mothering a nation of symbolic children. They, more than any of their more demure and reserved counterparts, exert overt power within the public domain. These are "mothers" who manage to rise to impressive heights of influence. We also included in our study a chapter on women we labeled, Unconventional Mothers. These mothers come into motherhood via unorthodox means. They cavort with divine beings, molest family members, and pose as prostitutes. They challenge and overcome the limits of patriarchy and achieve their goal of progeny in diverse and innovative ways.

Finally we analyzed the motherly role of God, exploring ways in which God acts as a mother to the children of Israel. Although the Bible predominantly gives God a masculine identity, the deity's more feminine, especially motherly, aspects emerge within biblical poetry. God is the "Ultimate Parent," exhibiting the best traits of both mother and father. We emphasized God's role as mother and suggested that many of the duties performed by the deity conjure up a human mother caring for her young. God's acting in the mother's role enhances her position, and lends support to our point that the mother has prominence and power within the Bible.

This study has been comprehensive as much as possible. We analyzed almost every maternal figure mentioned in the Bible and thematically categorized these women according to their stories and situations. In our study we encountered material that stimulated questions that went beyond the scope of this book. How has, for instance, the leadership style of the mother changed throughout the ages? Has it? Are there similarities in leadership between various mothers in history? Despite the shortcomings of the androcentric world of biblical mothers, can modern women nevertheless benefit somewhat from their experiences? Perhaps the present work will inspire other scholars to venture into this important and understudied subject. We hope that our research contributes to an engaging academic conversation among future exegetes and students of the Bible.

NOTE

1. Adrienne Rich, *On Lies, Secrets and Silence: Selected Prose 1966–1978* (New York: W.W. Norton & Company, 1980), 263.

Bibliography

Abot de Rabbi Nathan (ARNA)(ARNB) ed. Schechter, Solomon S. Vienna: D. Lippe, 1987.

Ackerman, Susan. "The Queen Mother and the Cult in Ancient Israel." In *Women in the Hebrew Bible*, ed. Alice Bach, 21–32. New York and London: Rutledge, 1999.

———. *Warrior, Dancer, Seductress, Queen: Women in Judges and Biblical Israel*. New York: Doubleday, 1998.

———. "And the Women Knead Dough: The Worship of the Queen of Heaven in 6th Judah." In *Gender and Difference in Ancient Israel*, ed. Peggy L. Day, 109–124. Minneapolis: Fortress Press, 1989.

Adler, Rachel. "A Mother In Israel: Aspects of the Mother Role in Jewish Myth." In *Beyond Androcentrism: New Essays on Women and Religion*, ed. R. M. Gross, 237–258. Missoula, Montana: Scholars Press, 1977.

Alter, Robert. *The Art of Biblical Narrative*. New York: Basic Books, 1981.

Amaru, Betsy Halpern. "Portraits of Biblical Women in Josephus' *Antiquities*." *JJS* 39 (1988): 143–170.

Amit, Yairah. "Am I Not More Devoted To You Than Ten Sons?" In *A Feminist Companion to Samuel and Kings*, ed. Athalya Brenner, 68–76. Sheffield Academic Press: Sheffield, England, 1994.

Anderson, Bernhard, W., "The Book of Esther." *The Interpreter's Bible*. Vol.III. New York: Abington Press, 1954.

Andreasen, N. A., "The Role of the Queen Mother in Israelite Society." *Catholic Bible Quarterly* 45 (1983): 179–94.

Arthur, Marylin B. "The Origins of the Western Attitude Toward Women." In *Women in the Ancient World, The Arethusa Papers*, ed. J. Peradatto, and J. P. Sullivan, 7–58. Albany: SUNY Press, 1984.

Aschkenasy, Nehama. *Eve's Journey: Feminine Images in Hebraic Literary Tradition*. Detroit: Wayne University Press, 1986.

Babylonian Talmud. Venice Edition. New York: Yam Ha-Talmud/Shulsinger Bros., 1948.

Bal, Mieke. *Death and Dissymmetry: The Politics of Coherence in the Book of Judges.* Chicago: University of Chicago Press, 1988.

Barr, James. "The Symbolism of Names in the Old Testament." *The Bulletin of the John Rylands Library* 62 (1969): 1–29.

Baskin, Judith R. "Introduction." *Jewish Women in Historical Perspective,* ed. Judith R. Baskin. Detroit: Wayne State University Press, 1991.

———. "Rabbinic Reflections on the Barren Wife." *Harvard Theological Review* 82 (1989): 101–114.

Bellis, Alice Ogden. *Helpmates Harlots Heroes, Women's Stories in the Hebrew Bible.* Louisville, Kentucky: Westminster/John Knox Press, 1994.

Ben-Barak, Zafrira, "The Status and Right of the Gebira." In *A Feminine Companion to Samuel and Kings,* ed. Athalya Brenner, 170–185. Sheffield, England: Sheffied Academic Press, (1994).

Berg, Sandra. *The Book of Esther.* Scholars Press: Missoula, 1979.

Bird, Phyllis. "The Harlot as Heroine: Narrative Art and Social Presupposition in Three Old Testament Texts." *Semeia* 46 (1989): 119–139.

Bloch, Ariel and Chana Bloch. *The Song of Songs: A New Translation with an Introduction and Commentary.* New York: Random House, 1951.

Boling, Robert G. *The Anchor Bible: Judges.* New York: Doubleday, 1975.

The Book of Legends, Sefer Ha-Aggadah, Legends from the Talmud and Midrash. ed. Hayim Nahman Bialik. Trans. William Braude. New York: Schocken Books Inc., 1992.

Bos, Johanna W. H. "Out of the Shadows: Genesis 38; Judges 4:17–22; Ruth 3." *Semeia* 42 (1988): 37–67.

Botterweck, Johannes G, and Ringgren Helmer, eds. *The Theological Dictionary of the Old Testament.* Vol 1. Grand Rapids, Michigan: Eerdmans Press, 1970–1972.

Boyarin, Daniel. *Carnal Israel: Reading Sex in Talmudic Culture.* Berkeley: University of California Press, 1993.

———. "Reading Androcentrism Against the Grain: Women, Sex and Torah Study," *Poetics Today* 12 (1991): 29–52.

Brenner Athalya, ed. *A Feminist Companion to Samuel and Kings.* Sheffield: Sheffield Academic Press, 1994.

Brenner, Athalya and Fontaine, Carole, eds. *A Feminist Companion to Reading the bible: Approaches, Methods and Strategies.* Sheffield, England: Sheffield Academic Press, 1997.

Bronner, Leila L. "Biblical Prophetesses through Rabbinic Lenses." *Judaism* 40 (1991): 171–183.

———. "The Changing Face of Woman from Bible to Talmud." *Shofar* 7 (1989): 34–47.

———. "Gynomorphic Imagery in Exilic Isaiah." *Dor Le Dor* [*The Jewish Quarterly*] 12 (1983/84): 71–76.

———. *The Stories of Elijah and Elisha.* Leiden: E. J. Brill, 1968.

———. *Sects and Separatism During the Second Jewish Commonwealth.* New York: Bloch Publishing Company, 1967.

Brooten, Bernadette J. *Women Leaders in the Ancient Synagogue: Inscriptional Evidence and Background Issues.* Brown Judaic Studies 36. Chico, CA: Scholar's Press, 1982.

Brown, Cheryl Anne. *No Longer Be Silent: First Century Jewish Portraits of Biblical Women.* Gender and the Biblical Tradition. Louisville: Westminster/John Knox Press, 1992.

Brown, Francis, S. R. Driver, and C. A. Briggs. *A Hebrew and English Lexicon of the Old Testament.* Oxford: Clarendon Press, 1951.

Callaway, Mary. *Sing, O Barren One: A Study in Comparative Midrash.* SBL Dissertation Series 91. Atlanta: Scholars Press, 1986.

Camp, Claudia V. *Wisdom and the Feminine in the Book of Proverbs.* Bible and Literature Series, no. 11. Sheffield, England: Almond Press, 1985.

Campbell, Edward F., Jr. *The Anchor Bible: Ruth.* New York: Doubleday, 1975.

Charles, R. H. *The Apocrypha and Pseudepigrapha of the Old Testament in English,* 2 Vols. Oxford: Clarendon Press, 1913. [Reprinted 1979–1983].

Charlesworth, James H. *The Old Testament Pseudepigrapha.* 2 Vols. Garden City, NY: Doubleday, 1983-5.

Cohen, Shaye J. D. *From the Maccabees to the Mishnah.* Library of Early Christianity. Philadelphia: Fortress, 1987.

Cohen, Shaye J. D. "Women in the Synagogues of Antiquity." *Conservative Judaism* 34 (1980): 23–29.

———. *From the Maccabees to the Mishnah.* Library of Early Christianity. Philadelphia: Westminster Press, 1987.

Crenshaw, J.L. *Samson: A Secret Betrayed, A Vow Ignored.* Atlanta: John Knox, 1978.

de Boer, P.A.H. *Fatherhood and Motherhood in Israelite and Judean Piety.* Leiden: E.J.Brill, 1974.

de Vaux, Roland. *Ancient Israel.* New York: McGraw-Hill, 1965 [Reprinted].

Daly Mary. *Beyond God the Father.* Boston: Beacon Press, 1973.

Day Peggy L. *Gender and Difference in Ancient Israel.* Minneapolis: Fortress Press, 1989.

Eliade, Mircea, ed. *Encyclopedia of Religion.* New York: MacMillan, 1987.

Encyclopedia Judaica. Jerusalem: Keter, 1971.

Encyclopedia Biblica. (Encyclopedia Mikra'it. [Hebrew]). Jerusalem: Instituti Bialik, 1955.

Encyclopedia Talmudit. [Hebrew]. Jerusalem: Yad Harav Herzog Press, 1982.

Epstein, I., ed. *Babylonian Talmud.* London: The Soncino Press, 1952.

Epstein, Louis M. *Sex Laws and Customs in Judaism.* Revised edition. New York: Ktav, 1987.

Eskenazi, Tamara C. "Out From the Shadows: Biblical Woman in the Post-Exilic Era." *JSOT* 54 (1992): 25–43.

Even-Shoshan, A. *A New Concordance of the Old Testament.* Jerusalem: Kiryat Sefer Publishing House, Ltd., 1985.

Exum, J. Cheryl. "Deborah." *Harper's Bible Dictionary.* San Francisco: Harper & Row, 1985.

———. *Fragmented Women*. Valley Forge, PA: Trinity Press Int., 1993

———. "Promise and Fulfillment: Narrative Art in Judges 13." *Journal of Biblical Literature* 99 (1980): 43–59.

———. "The 'Mothers of Israel,' The Patriarchal Narratives from a Feminist Perspective." *Bible Review* 2 (1986): 60–67.

Fewel, Danna Nolan. "Judges." In *The Women's Bible Commentary*, ed by Carol A. Newsom and Sharon H. Ringe, 73–83. Louisville, Kentucky: Westminister/John Knox, 1992.

Finkelstein, Louis. *Halachah and Agadah*. New York: Jewish Theological Seminary of America, 1960.

Fitzmyer, Joseph A. *The Genesis Apocryphon of Qumran Cave 1*. Rome: Pontifical Institute, 1966.

Fox, Michael V. *The Song of Songs and the Ancient Egyptian Love Songs*. Madison, Wisconsin: University of Wisconsin Press, 1985.

Freedman, R. David. "Woman, A Power Equal to Man." *Biblical Archaelogist Review* 9 (1983): 56–58.

Friedman, Theodore. "The Shifting Role of Women, from Bible to Talmud." *Judaism* 36 (1987): 479–487.

Fuchs, Esther. "The Literary Characterization of Mothers and Sexual Politics in the Hebrew Bible." *Semeia* 46 (1989): 151–166.

———. "'For I Have the Way of Women': Deception, Gender, and Ideology in Biblical Narrative." *Semeia* 42 (1988): 68–83.

———. *Sexual Politics In The Biblical Narrative, Reading The Hebrew Bible As A Woman*. Sheffield: Sheffield Academic Press Ltd., 2000.

Ginzberg, Louis. *Legends of the Jews*. 7 Vols. Philadelphia: Jewish Publication Society, 1946

Goldfeld, Anne. "Women as Sources of Torah in the Rabbinic Tradition." In *The Jewish Woman*, ed. by Elizabeth Kolton, 257–271. New York: Schocken Books, 1976.

Goldman, S. *Esther: Introduction and Commentary*. The Five Megilloth: Hebrew Text, English Translation and Commentary. London: Soncino Press, 1946.

Gordis, Robert. "Love, Marriage, and Business in the Book of Ruth: A Chapter in Hebrew Customary Law." In *Light Unto My Path: Old Testament Studies in Honor of Jacob M. Myers*, ed. by H. N. Bream, R. D. Heim, and C. A. Moore, 241–264. Philadelphia: Temple University, 1974.

Gross, Moshe D. *Ozar HaAgadah*. 3 Vols. [Hebrew]. Jerusalem: Mosad HaRav Kook, 1960.

Gruber, Mayer. *The Motherhood of God and Other Studies*. Atlanta: Scholars Press, 1992.

Hackett, Jo Ann. "Women's Studies and the Hebrew Bible." In *The Future of Biblical Studies: The Hebrew Scriptures*, ed. by Richard Elliott Friedman and H. G. M. Williamson, 141–164. SBL Semeia Studies. Atlanta: Scholars Press, 1987.

Halpern, B. *The First Historians: The Hebrew Bible and History*. San Francisco: Harper & Row, 1988.

Harrington, Daniel J. "Pseudo-Philo." *The Old Testament Pseudepigrapha*. Vol. 2, ed. J. H. Charlesworth, 297–378. Garden City, NY: Doubleday, 1985.

Harrington, Daniel J. and Saldarini, Anthony J. *Targum Jonathan of the Former Prophets: Introduction, Translation, and Notes.* Wilmington, Del.: Michael Glazier, 1987.
Harris, Rivkah. "Independent Women in Ancient Mesopotamia?" In *Women's Earliest Records: From Ancient Egypt and Western Asia,* ed. B. S. Lesko, 145–156. Atlanta: Scholar's Press, 1989.
Hartmann, D. *Das Buch Ruth in der Midrasch-Litteratur.* Leipzig, 1901.
Heinemann, Joseph. *'Aggadot v'Toldoteihen.* [Hebrew]. [*Aggadah and Its Development*]. Jerusalem: Keter, 1974.
Herbert, A.S. *Isaiah 40–66, Cambridge Bible Commentary.* ed. Ackroyd et al. London: Cambridge University Press, 1975.
Herford, Travers V. *Talmud and Apocrypha.* New York: Ktav Publishing, 1971.
Hesiod. *The Works and Days, Theogony, and the Shield of Herakles.* Trans. R. Lattimore. Ann Arbor: University of Michigan Press, 1959.
Homer. *The Odyssey.* Book 21. Harvard Classics Edition, 1909.
Hurwitz S.Y. "R. Eliezer ben Horkanos and Women's Education." *Hashahar* 11 (1883): 437–41.
Hyman, Aharon. *Toldoth Tannaim Ve'Amoraim.* London: Express Press, 1910.
Hyman, Aharon. *Torah, HaKethubah,Ve-ha-Messurah,* 3 Vols. Tel Aviv: Dvir, 1979.
Ilan, Tal. *Jewish Women in Greco-Roman Palestin.* Peabody, MA:Hendrickson, 1996
———. *'Mine & Yours are Hers': Retrieving Women's History from Rabbinic Literature.* Leiden: Brill, 1997.
———. *Integrating Women into Second Temple History.* Peabody, MA: Hendrickson, 2001.
Interpreter's Bible. 6 Vols. ed. George A. Buttrick, et al. Nashville/New York: Abingdon, 1952–1956.
Interpreter's Dictionary of the Bible. 4 Vols. Nashville/New York: Abingdon, 1962.
Jastrow, M. *A Dictionary of the Targumim, the Talmud Babli and Yerushalmi, and the Midrashic Literature.* New York: Pardes Publishing House, 1950.
Jewish Encyclopedia. New York and London: Funk and Wagnalls, 1904
Jones, Bruce W. "Two Misconceptions About the Book of Esther," in *Studies in The Book of Esther,* ed. Carey Moore, 437–447. New York: Ktav Publishing, 1982.
Josephus, Flavius. 9 vols. Loeb Classical Library. London: William Heinemann. Vol. 4, *Jewish Antiquities, Books* 1–4, trans. H. St. J. Thackeray, 1928. Vol. 5, *Jewish Antiquities, Books* 5–8, trans. H. St. J. Thackeray and Ralph Marcus, 1927.
Josephus, Flavius: *Complete Works.* Trans. William Whiston. 1867. Reprint. Grand Rapids: Kregel Publications, 1960.
Kaiser, Barbara Bakke. "Poet as 'Female Impersonator': The Image of Daughter Zion as Speaker in Biblical Poems of Suffering." *The Journal of Religion* 67 (1987): 164–182.
Kee, Howard Clark "The Testaments of the Twelve Patriarchs." *The Old Testament Pseudepigrapha,* Vol. I, ed. James H. Charlesworth, 775–828. Garden City, NY: Doubleday, 1983.
Köhler, Ludwig, and W. Baumgartner. *Lexicon in Veteris Testamenti Libros* and *Supplementum ad Lexicon.* Leiden: E. J. Brill, 1958.

Köhler, Ludwig (*Old Testament Theology*, trans. A.S. Todd [Philadelphia: Westminster Press, 1957], 251, n. 153

Kaufmann Kohler, *Jewish Theology* Cincinnati: Riverdale Press, 1943.

Koltuv, Barbara Black. *The Book of Lilith.* York Beach, Maine: Nicolas-Hays, 1987.

Kraemer, Ross S. *Her Share of the Blessings: Women's Religion Among Pagans, Jews, and Christians in the Greco-Roman World.* Oxford: Oxford University Press, 1992.

Kraemer, Ross S. *Maenads, Martyrs, Matrons, Monastics.* Philadelpha: Fortress Press, 1987.

Kraemer, Ross S. "Women in the Religions of the Greco-Roman World." *Religious Studies Review* 9 (1983): 127–139.

Kraemer, Ross S. "The Diaspora World of Late Antiquity" in *Jewish Women: Historical Perspective*, ed. Judith R. Baskin Detroit: Wayne State University Press, 1991.

Kugel, James L. *In Potiphar's House.* San Francisco: Harper Collins, 1990.

———. "Two Introductions to Midrash." In *Midrash and Literature*, ed. G. H. Hartman and S. Budick, 77–104. New Haven: Yale University Press, 1986. Laffey Alice, An Introduction to the Old Testament, Philadelphia: Fortress Press, 1988.

Kuzmack, Linda. "Aggadic Approaches to Biblical Women." *The Jewish Woman*, ed. E. Kohn, 248–256. New York: Schocken Books, 1976.

Laetsch, Theo, *Bible Commentary Jeremiah.* St. Louis, Missouri: Concordia Publishing House, 1965.

Lauterbach, J.Z.,ed. *Mekilta de-Rabbi Ishmael* 3 Vols. [Hebrew and English]. Schiff Library of Jewish Classics. Philadelphia: Jewish Publication Society of America, 1933–1935.

Leibowitz, Nehama.*Studies in the Book of Genesis.* Trans. Aryeh Newman. Jerusalem: World Zionist Organization, 1972.

Lerner, Berel D. "And He Shall Rule Over Thee." *Judaism* 37 (1988): 446–449.

Levine, Amy-Jill, ed. *Women Like This: New Perspectives on Jewish Women in the Greaco Roman World.* Atlanta: Scholars Press, 1991.

Loewe, Raphael. *The Position of Women in Judaism.* London: SPCK, 1966.

Maimonides, M. *Guide to the Perplexed.* Trans. S. Pines. Chicago: University of Chicago Press: 1963.

Maimonides, M. *Mishneh Torah.* New York: Shulsinger Bros., 1947.

Margulies, M., ed. *Midrash Wa-Yiqra' Rabbah*, 5 Vols. Jerusalem: Wahrmann, 1953–60; Reprinted 1972.

Mazar, Benjamin, ed. *Views of the Biblical World.* Chicago: Jordan Publications, Inc., 1959.

Meiselman, Moshe. *Jewish Woman in Jewish Law.* New York: Ktav Publishing House, 1978.

Melzer, Feivel. "Ruth." In *The Five Scrolls.* [Hebrew]. Jerusalem: Mosad Harav Kook, 1973.

Meyers, Carol. *Discovering Eve: Ancient Israelite Women in Context.* Oxford: Oxford University Press, 1988.

———. *Women in Scripture*, Meyers, ed. Grand Rapids, Michigan: Houghton Mifflin, 2000.

———. "'To Her Mother's House': Considering a Counterpart to the Israelite *Bêt 'ab*." In *The Bible and the Politics of Exegesis*, ed. David Jobling, Peggy L. Day, and Gerald T. Sheppard, 39–51. Cleveland: Pilgrim Press, 1991.

———. "Returning Home: Ruth 1.8 and the Gendering of the Book of Ruth," In *A Feminist Companion to Ruth*, ed. Athalya Brenner, 85–114. Sheffield: Sheffield Academic Press, 1993.

Meyers, Carol "Gender Imagery in the Song of Songs." *Hebrew Annual Review* 10 (1986): 209–223.

Midrash Bereshit Rabba. 3 Vols. [Hebrew]. ed. J. Theodor and C. Albeck. Jerusalem: Wahrmann Books, 2nd ed., 1965.

Midrash Bereshit Rabbati, ed. C. Albeck. Jerusalem: Mekize Nirdamim, 1940.

Midrash Mishle. ed. S. Buber. Vilna, 1893. Reprinted in Israel, 1973.

Midrash Pesiqta Rabbati. ed. M. Friedmann (Ish-Shalom). Vienna, 1888.

Midrash Rabbah. 10 Vols. ed. H. Freedman and M. Simon. London: Soncino Press, 3rd edition, 1983.

Miqra'ot Gedolot. New York: Pardes, 1951.

Mishnah. Ed. by H. Danby. Oxford: Oxford University Press, 1933. Reprinted in 1983.

Montefiore, C. G., and H. Loewe, eds. *The Rabbinic Anthology*. Meridian Books, 1970.

Moon, Beverly. "Archtypes." *The Encyclopedia of Religion*. Vol. I. ed. Mircea Eliade, 379–382. New York: MacMillan Publishers, 1997.

Moore, Carey A. *Studies in the Book of Esther*. New York: Ktav Publishing House, 1980.

———. *Daniel, Esther, and Jeremiah: The Additions*. The Anchor Bible. New York: Doubleday, 1977.

———. *Esther: A New Translation with Introduction and Commentary*. The Anchor Bible. New York: Doubleday, 1971.

Moore, George F. *A Critical and Exegetical Commentary on Judges*. Edinburgh: T&T Clark, 1918.

Neusner, Jacob. *The Talmud of the Land of Israel. (Yerushalmi)*. Chicago: The University of Chicago Press, 1989.

———. *The Mishnah: A New Translation*. New Haven: Yale, 1988.

———. *Midrash in Context: Exegesis in Formative Judaism*. Philadelphia: Fortress Press, 1983.

———. *The Tosefta*. [Order Nashim; Translated from the Hebrew]. New York: Ktav, 1979.

Niditch, Susan. "Portrayals of Women in the Hebrew Bible." In *Jewish Women in Historical Perspective*, ed. Judith Baskin, 25–42. Detroit: Wayne State University Press, 1991.

———. *Underdogs and Trickster: A Prelude to Biblical Folklore*. San Francisco: Harper and Row, 1987.

Ortner, Sherry B. "Is Female to Male as Nature Is to Culture?" In *Woman, Culture, & Society*, ed. Michelle Zimbalist Rosaldo and Louise Lamphere, 67–88. Stanford: Stanford University Press, 1974.

Palestinian Talmud. Krotoshin edition. New York: Yam Ha-Talmud/Shulsinger Bros., 1948.
Pardes, Ilana, *Countertraditions in the Bible: A Feminist Approach*. Cambridge: Harvard University Press, 1992.
Patai, Raphael. *The Hebrew Goddess*. New York: Avon Books, 1978.
Paton,, Lewis B. *The Book of Esther: Critical and Exegetical Commentary*. Edinburgh: T&T Clark, 1976.
Pederson, Johs. *Israel, Its Life and Culture*. 2 Vols. London: Oxford University Press, 1959.
Peritz, Ismar J. "Woman in the Ancient Hebrew Cult." *JBL* 17 (1898): 111–148.
Pesikta de-Rab Kahana. Trans. W. G. Braude and I. J. Kapstein. Philadelphia: Jewish Publication Society, 1975.
Pesiqta de Rav Kahana, According to an Oxford Manuscript with Variants from all Known Manuscripts and Genizoth Fragments and Parallel Passages with Commentary and Introduction. Ed. by Bernard [Dov] Mandelbaum. New York: Jewish Theological Seminary, 1962.
Pesiqta de Rav Kahana. ed. Solomon Buber. Lwow: 1868. Reprinted 1963.
Pesikta Rabbati. Tran. William G. Braude. New Haven: Yale University Press, 1968.
Phillips, John A. *Eve, The History of an Idea*. San Francisco: Harper and Row, 1984.
Philo. *Philo I-X*. Tran. F. H. Colson and G. H. Whitaker. Loeb Classical Library. London: William Heinemann, 1929–53.
Pirqei Rabbi Eliezer. Warsaw (based on Bomberg) 1660. Reprinted in Israel, 1978.
Plaskow, Judith. "Blaming the Jews for the Birth of Patriarchy," *Lilith* 7 (1980): 11–13.
Pope, M.H. *Song of Songs*. Garden City, N.Y.:Doubleday, 1977.
Pritchard, J.B., ed. "Epic of Gilgamesh." *Ancient Near Eastern Texts*. Princeton: Princeton University Press, 1955.
Prusak, Bernard P. "Women: Seductive Siren and Source of Sin?" *Religion and Sexism: Images of Woman in the Jewish and Christian Traditions*, ed. by Rosemary R. Ruether, 89–116. New York: Simon and Schuster, 1974.
Rosaldo, Michelle Z., and Louise Lamphere, eds. *Women, Culture and Society: A Theoretical Overview*. Stanford, CA: Stanford University Press, 1974.
Russell. Letty M, ed. *Feminist Interpretation of the Bible*. Philadelphia: Westminster, 1985.
Rosenberg, A. J. "Ruth." In *The Five Megillot*. Revised Edition. London: Soncino, 1984.
Safrai, Shmuel. *The Jewish People in the Days of the Second Temple*. Tel Aviv: Am Oved, 1970.
———. "Was There a Woman's Section in the Synagogue of Antiquity?" *Tarbiz* 32 [Hebrew]. (1963): 329–338.
Saldarini, Anthony J. *The Fathers According to Rabbi Nathan*. Studies in Judaism in Late Antiquity 11. Leiden: E. J. Brill, 1975.
Sarna, Nahum A. *Understanding Genesis*. New York: Jewish Theological Seminary/McGraw-Hill, 1966.
———. *The JPS Torah Commentary, Genesis*. New York: Jewish Publication Society, 1989.

Sasson, Jack M. *Ruth: A New Translation with a Philological Commentary*. Baltimore: Johns Hopkins, 1979.
Schuller, Eileen. "Women of the Exodus in Biblical Retellings of the Second Temple." In *Gender and Difference in Ancient Israel*, ed. Peggy L. Day, 178–194. Minneapolis: Fortress Press, 1989.
Segal, Moshe Z. *The Complete Book of Ben Sira*. [Hebrew]. Jerusalem: Mosad Bialik, 1956.
———. *Ruth: Introduction to the Bible*, Vol 3. [Hebrew]. Jerusalem: Kiryat Sefer, 1955.
Shargent Karla G. "Living on the Edge: The Liminality of Daughters in Genesis to 2 Samuel." In *A Feminist Companion to Samuel and Kings*, ed. Athalya Brenner, 22–42. Sheffield: Sheffield Academic Press, 1994.
Shaw, Harry. *Dictionary of Literary Terms*. New York: McGraw-Hill Book Co., 1972.
Shoub, Myra Nelson, "Jewish Women's History :Development of a Critical Methodolgy," *Conservative Judaism XXXV*, no.2 (1982): 33–46.
Shisha Sidre ha-Mishnah. ed. C. Albeck, 6 vols. Jerusalem: Bialik Institute, 1958.
Sifra De'Vey Rav, Sifrei D'Vey Rav. M. Friedmann (Ish-Shalom), ed. Breslau, rpt. Israel: 1923.
Sigal,Lillian. "Models of Love and Hate," *Daughters of Sarah* 16, 2, 1990.
Skehan, Patrick W. and Alexander A. Di Lella, *The Wisdom of Ben Sira*. The Anchor Bible. New York: Doubleday, 1987.
Skinner, J., ed., *A Critical and Exegetical Commentary on Genesis*, The International Critical Commentary. Edinburgh: T. & T. Clark, 1969.
Sly, Dorothy. *Philo's Perception of Women*. Brown Judaic Studies 209, ed. J. Neusner, et. al. Atlanta: Scholar's Press, 1990.
Smith, Henry Preserved. *A Critical and Exegetical Commentary on The Books of Samuel*, The International Critical Commentary. Edinburgh: T. &. T. Clark, 1899, rpt. 1912.
Smith, L. P.*The Interpreters Bible* , vol. 2. New York: Abingdon Press, 1954.
Soloveitchik, Joseph D. "The Lonely Man of Faith." *Tradition* 7 (1965): 5–67.
Speiser, E. A. *Genesis*. The Anchor Bible. Garden City, NY: Doubleday, 1964.
Sperber, A. *The Bible in Aramaic*, 5 vols. Leiden: E. J. Brill, 1973.
Sullivan, J. P. "Women in Classical Literature," an unpublished source book.
Sussman, Linda S. "Workers and Drones; Labor, Idleness and Gender Definition in Hesiod's Beehive." *Women in the Ancient World: The Arethusa Papers*, ed. John Peradotto and J. P. Sullivan. Albany: SUNY Press, 1984.
Swidler, Leonard. *Women in Judaism: The Status of Women in Formative Judaism*. Metuchen, NJ: Scarecrow Press, 1976.
Talmud of the Land of Israel, ed. J. Neusner, vol. 1, *Berachot*, trans. Tsvee Zahavy. Chicago: University of Chicago Press, 1989.
Talmud Yerushalmi. Jerusalem: Academy of the Hebrew Language. 2001.
Terrien,Samuel, "Toward a Biblical Theology of Womenhood," *Religion in Life* Vol. 42 (1973): 323–333.
The Tosefta. ed. M.S. Zuckermandel. Jerusalem: Wahrmann, 1962–63.

The Tosefta According to Codex Vienna, with Variants from Codices Erfurt, Genizah Mss. and Editio Princeps (Venice 1521). Vol 3, Pt. 2: *Nasim: Sota, Gittin, Qiddusin*. ed. Saul Lieberman. New York: Jewish Theological Seminary, 1973.

Trenchard, Warren C. *Ben Sira's View of Women*. Brown Judaica Series 38. Chico, CA: Scholars Press, 1982.

Trible, Phyllis. "Eve." *Harper's Bible Dictionary*. San Francisco: Harper & Row, 1985.

———. *Texts of Terror: Literary-Feminist Readings of Biblical Narratives*. Philadelphia: Fortress Press, 1984.

———. *God and the Rhetoric of Sexuality*. Philadelphia: Fortress, 1978.

———. "Depatriarchalizing in Biblical Interpretation." *JAAR* 12 (1973): 39–41.

Urbach, Ephraim. *The Sages: Their Concepts and Beliefs*. Jerusalem: Magnes Press, 1975.

Valler, Shulamit. *Women and Womanhood in Talmud*. Atlanta: Scholars Press, 1999.

Van der Toorn, Karel. "Female Prostitution in Payment of Vows in Ancient Israel." *JBL* 108 (1989): 193–205.

van Wijk-Bos, Johanna W.H. *Reformed and Feminist: A Challenge to the Church*. Louisville, Ky.: Westminster/John Knox, 1991.

Von Rad, Gerhardt. *Genesis*. The Old Testament Library. Philadelphia: Westminster, 1972.

Vos, Clarence J. *Woman in Old Testament Worship*. Delft: Judels & Brinkman, 1968.

Wakeman, Mary K. "Sacred Marriage." *JSOT* 22 (1982): 21–31.

Wegner, Judith R. "The Image and Status of Women in Classical Rabbinic Judaism." *Jewish Women in Historical Perspective*, ed. J. R. Baskin, 68–93. Detroit: Wayne State University Press, 1991.

———. *Chattel or Person? The Status of Women in the Mishnah*. New York and Oxford: Oxford University Press, 1988.

———. "The Image of Woman in Philo." In *SBL Seminar Papers*, ed. K.H.Richards, 551–63. Chico, CA: Scholars Press, 1982.

Weiss, Avi. *Women at Prayer: A Halakhic Analysis of Women's Prayer Groups*. Hoboken, NJ: Ktav, 1990.

Wertheimer, S. ed. *Batei Midrashot*. Jerusalem: Ketav Yad Yosef, 1982[reprint].

Westenholz, Joan G. "Tamar, Qedesa, Qadistu, and Sacred Prostitution in Mesopotamia." *HTR* 82 (1989): 245–65.

Westermann, C., *Isaiah 40–66*. Philadephia: Westminster Press, SCM Press Ltd., 1969.

Wintermute, Orville S. "Jubilees." In *The Old Testament Pseudepigrapha*, vol. 2, ed. J. H. Charlesworth, 35–142. Garden City, NJ: Doubleday, 1983.

Yalkut Shimoni. Monson, 2 vols. Jerusalem, 1962.

Young, R. *Young's Analytical Concordance to the Bible*. Grand Rapids, MI: William B. Eerdmans Publishing Company, 1970.

Young, Serinity, ed. *Encyclopedia of Women and World Religion*. 2 Vols. New York: Macmillan Reference USA, 1999.

Zakovitch, Yair. *Ruth: Introduction and Commentary*. Mikra LeYisra'el: A Bible Commentary for Israel, ed. M. Greenberg, and S. Ahituv. Tel Aviv and Jerusalem: Am Oved Publishers/Magnes Press, 1990. [Hebrew].

Zohar. H. Sperling, and M. Simon, trans. London and New York: Soncino Press, 1984.

Zornberg, Avivah Gottlieb. *Genesis: The Beginning of Desire*. Philadelphia: Jewish Publication Society, 1995.

Index

Abimelech, 37
Abishag, 51
Abraham, 5, 7, 12
Absalom, 44, 65, 66
Ackerman, Susan, 45, 48, 56n7, 57n19
Adah, 4–5
Adam, 2, 3
Adonijah, 50, 51
Ahab, 53
Ahinoam, 65
Ahithopel, 57n22
Akedah, 7–8
'alman, 114
'amas, 111
Ammonites, 95
Amnon, 44, 65–66
Amram, 63
ancient Israel, women's ability to achieve power in, viii
Andreasen, Niels-Erik, 48, 57n14
Asa, 53
'asah, 109
Asherah cult, 53, 107
Athalya, 54–55
authority, vii

Bal, Mieke, 29, 40n12n15
Barak, 80, 82

barrenness, 5, 18, 39; aspects of motif, 26–27; Hannah's, 31, 33; Rachel's 20; Shunammite woman unbothered by, 34, 39
Bathsheba, 48, 50–52
Bellis, Alice, 28, 40n5
Ben-Barak, Zafrira, 48, 57n16
Benjamin, 20
Benoni, naming of, 19–20
Bible: difference in role and responsibility between men and women, 19; females' experience used metaphorically in, 74n3; feminist approaches to, viii; God the mother in, separated from erotic role, 61; male-centered tone of, viii; metaphorical daughter used in, 60; naming in, 2, 49. *See* naming; parenting in, 61; rarely recording loyalty between women, 68; rarely recording woman's demise, 84–85
biblical interpretation, Huldah as innovator in, 89
biblical mothers: authority of, 43; cannibalizing sons, 38; causes of evil visited on sons, 37; daughters' finding safety in, 70; devoted to children's protection and longevity, 5; divergence

among, 39; during chaotic historical period, 38–39; fear of weapons, 4, 5; finding power through mother role, 35; in Genesis, ix–x, 1–22, 119–20; high proportion of appearance in Song of Songs, 72; idealized wise figure, 42–43; influence on child's destiny, 36; involvement in children's education, 43; irregular marital status of, 37; Israelites juxtaposed with foreigners, 30; mating with divine beings, 96–97; metaphorical examples, 78–93; methodology for studying, xi–xii; namers of children, 2; names related to natural imagery, 11–12; negative characters, 26, 37–38, 39; nurturing a nation, x; often unnamed, in stories of daughters, 62; power to dedicate sons to holy service, 32; protecting offspring, 6–7; single-minded purpose of, 22; status and power of, vii, viii; symbolic mothers, x–xi; unconventional, xi, xiii n9, 95–104; uniqueness of, ix; unofficial power of, 13–14; used to convey wisdom, 46; widening scope of political and cultural influence, 42; wise, non-royal, 44; "wise woman" stories, 44–47
biblical women, function related to patriarchy, vii
Bilhah, 20, 21
birth: joy of, 4, 6; as miracle, 5
Bloch, Ariel, 71, 72
Bloch, Chana, 71, 72
Boaz, 70
Brenner, Athalya, 37, 41n28, 57n13, 83
brothers, as agents for female relatives, 64–67

Camp, Claudia, 43, 44, 56n3
cannibalism, 38
childbirth, 3
childless widowhood, 102, 103. *See also* levirate marriage

children, marriage of, involvement of parents in, 61
conception, source of social superiority, 6
coronation, 52–53

daughters: biblical portrayal of, 61–62; metaphorical, 60–61; relations to mothers, 120. *See* mother-daughter relationships
daughters of Lot, 97–101
David, 46–47, 50, 66–67
Deborah, x, 78–82, 92
deception stories, 103
Delilah, 28, 29
Dinah, 63–65, 67, 68, 71
divine beings, mating with biblical mothers, 96–97

Eli, 31–32
Elisha, in Shunammite story, 34–35
Endor, see *Witch* (Necromancer)
Er, naming of, 101
Esau, 13, 14–15
Eshet Hayil, 43–44
Esther, 79, 85–87
Eve, 1, 2–4, 21
Evil-morodoch, 54
Exodus, story of, informing maternal relationship between God and Israel, 107–8
Exum, Cheryl, xiiin6, 77n43

families, mothers involved in destiny of, 1, 32, 35, 36, 43
family line, men's concern with, 18
female religious participation, 40n18
Fewell, Donna, 29, 39n11
Frymer-Kensky, Tikva, ix, 13, 80, 82, 93n6n12, 99, 105n6
Fuchs, Esther, xiiin6

Gehazi, 34, 35
Genesis Rabba, 100
gevirah, 48, 53, 54

Gibeonites, 47
God: birthing imagery related to, 109–11; depicted as mother giving birth, 60; maternal imagery used for love of, 113–14; as mother to daughter Israel, 59, 60–61; as motherly and fatherly love, 111–13; motherly role of, 106–15, 121; not limited by gender, 61, 108–9; response to Hagar and Ishmael, 10
gynomorphic imagery, biblical scholars' inability to cope with, 113–15

Hagar, 5, 9–11
Hammurabi, laws of, 23n14
Hamutal, 53–54
Hannah, x, 26, 31–34, 39
hannun, 113
Hatshepsut, 48, 57n15
Hephzibah, significance of name, 77n40
hesed, 70
Hillel, 81
historical records, limitations of, viii
hokhmah, 42
Hosea, on Jacob's treatment of Esau, 16
Huldah, 79, 87–89, 93
husbandry, 11–12

Ilan, Tal, xiiin4, 13
incest, 63, 65–66, 98–99
Isaac, 5, 6, 7–8, 12, 13, 14, 15
Isaiah, using birth images, 109–10
Ishmael, 5, 6, 7, 10–11
Israel: daughter of, x; as daughter to mother God, 59, 60–61, 107–8; incompetence of male leaders, 79–80

Jabal, 5
Jabez, naming of, 36
Jacob, 8–9, 12–15, 17–22, 64–65, 67
Jedidah, 88, 94n22
Jehoahaz, 53–54
Jehoiakin, 54
Jephthah, 37

Jeremiah, 16, 21–22, 109–10
Jeroboam, 49
Jezebel, 53, 54
Joab, 44, 45
Jochebed, 62, 63
Johnson, Miriam, 11, 24n26
Joseph, 19
Josephus, 91–92
Josiah, 88
Jubal, 5
Judah, xi, 101, 102

Kaiser, Barbara Bakke, 74n3
kiss, 17

Laban, 15
Lady Knowledge, 56n2
Lamech, 4–5
Leah, 5, 16–19, 63–64
Lemuel, 51–52
Levi, 64–65
levirate marriage, 65–66, 69–70, 101, 102, 103
Lot, xi, 97–101
Lot's daughters, 104

Maacah, 53, 65
Manasseh, 49
mandrakes, episode of, 19
Manoah, 27
matriarchs, references to, 115
metaphorical mothers, 78–93, 120
Meyers, Carol, 40n13, 75n12
mezachek, 6
Micah, 37–38
Michal, 57n11
Miriam, 62–63, 79, 83–85, 92–93
Moabites, 95
Mordecai, 86, 87
Moses, 12, 83, 107–8
mother-daughter relationships, x, 59, 62, 68–69, 73
mother goddess figures, Near Eastern mythology, 107

motherhood, pursuit of, 46–47, 100–101
mothering, ix
"mother in Israel," 45, 78–79, 80, 82, 92
Mother of Prayer, Hannah viewed as, 34
mothers: God in role of, xi, 106–15; metaphorical, 78–93; representing home, 15; unconventional, 120–21. *See also* biblical mothers, unnamed mothers
"mother's house," use of phrase, 71–72
mother-son relationships, ix–x, 50–51, 53

namegivers, gender of, 23n8
naming: Benoni, 19–20; in Bible, 2, 3–4, 49; biblical mothers as namers of children, 2; biblical mothers of daughters often unnamed, 62; Eve's sons, 3–4; gender of namegivers, 23n8; Hagar, 10–11; Hannah, 33; Hephzibah, 77n.40; importance of, ix–x, 35–36; Ishmael, 10–11; Jabez, 36; Joseph, 19; Judah's sons, 101; Leah's sons, 18; Lot, 98; of queen mothers, 49–50; Rachel's sons, 19–20; Rebecca, 11–12; related to natural imagery, 11–12; Samson, 28; Samuel, 32; Sarah, 8–9; significance of, 82, Tamar, 102
Naomi, 67–70, 72
national mothers, 83–87
Near Eastern goddess creation stories, 23n7
Nefertiti, 57n15
Nehushta, 53, 54
Nephillim, 95, 96–97, 104, 104n1
Niditch, Susan, 64, 103–4

Obed, 69
Onan, naming of, 101
Otwell, John, xiiin5

parent-child instructions, 61–62
Peninnah, 33

people, personified as daughter, 60
personal prayer, Hannah as patron of, 89
power, vii, 19
Pseudo-Philo, 37, 40n8, 81
Purim, Esther's role in, 86–87, 89

queen mothers, 47–55, 56, 120

Rachel, 5, 16–22, 25n46
Rahab, 79, 87, 89–91, 93
rahamim, 113
rahum, 113
Rashi, on Reuben, 20
Rebecca, 5, 8, 11–17, 21, 71, 72
rehem, 113
Reuben, 18, 19, 20
Rich, Adrienne, 119, 121
Rizpah, 46–47
Ruth, 67–70, 72, 99
Ruth, book of: similarities with Song of Songs, 71–72; sociological elements of narrative, 69–70

Samson, 27–30
Samuel, 32–33
Sarah, 1, 5–10, 13, 21
Satan, 7
Saul, 91–92
shegal, 52
shekinah, 112
Shelah, naming of, 101
Shunammite woman, x, 26, 34
Simeon, 64–65, 75–76n18
Sisera, mother of, 37
social power, types of, vii–viii
Sodom, 97–98, 100
Solomon, 50–53
song of Lamech, 23
Song of Songs: similarities with book of Ruth, 71–72; woman's relationship to mother and brothers portrayed in, 70–73
Speiser, E., 24n37, 98

Tamar, xi, 44, 63, 65–67, 68, 69, 71, 96, 101–4
Tanna Debe Eliyahu, 81
Targum Jonathan, 81
Themech, 37
theophanies, 9, 10, 14–15, 27
Tiy, 57n15
Trible, Phyllis, 8, 11, 109, 113
Tubal-Cain, 5

unassigned power, vii–viii
unnamed mothers: mother of Abimelech, 37; mother of Ahaz, 49; mother of Jabez, 35–36; mother of Jehoram, 49; mother of Jephthah, 37; mother of Lemuel, 51–52; mother of Micah, 38; mother of Samson, x, 27–28, 29, 39
Ur-Nammu, 23n14

Vashti, Queen, 85

Westermann, Claus, 114
Wisdom, female personification of, 42, 43–44
Wisdom stories, 55–56
"wise women," 44–47, 55, 120
wise woman of Abel, 45
Witch (Necromancer) of Endor, 79, 87, 91–92, 93
womb, imagery in Samson story, 29–30
women: as leaders, 46, 82; public participation of, 80; of valor, 90

Yochebed, 83

Zedekiah, 53–54
Zeruah, 49
Zillah, 4–5
Zilpah, 21
Zion, giving birth, 111

Index of Scriptural References

Genesis
1–11	97	17:15	24n22
1:7, 16	109	19:13	97
2:19–20	2	19:14	6
2:21–22	2	19:16–18	97
2:23	3	19:30–38	98–99
3:16	3	19:33	100
3:20	2	20:1–18	103
3:21	109	21:1	5
4:1	3	21:7	5
4:1–31	64	21:9	6
4:23–24	4	21:9–13	14
4:26	3	21:11–21	7
6	96	21:12	7
6:1–4	96	21:15	10
6:2	96	21:18–21	10
6:4	96	22:2	77n42
11:29	5	24	76n28
11:30	5	24:1	74n1
14b–21	10	24:28	72, 75n12
15	24n30	24:55	72
16:3	24n23	24:55–59	67
16:6–16	5	24:58	12
16:7–15	9	24:67	8, 72
16:11	10	25:22	13
16:11–12	10	26:8	6
16:13	11	26:22–24	14
17:4	24n22	26:22–28	13
		26:67	13

27	17	48:7	18		
27:1	15	49:3ff	20		
27:5–6	16	49:4	25n44		
27:6–14	15	49:5–7	64–65		
27:8–16	103	66:7–9	60		
27:13	14				
27:46	14	**Exodus**			
28:5	14	1:15–21	103		
28:45	15	1:22	63		
29:1–2	17	2	62, 63		
29:1–12	12	2:1–10	83		
29:9–11	17	2:10	62		
29:16	17	2:17	12, 24n39		
29:16–17	17	4:14	62		
29:20	17	6:20	62, 63		
29:31–35	25n41	15:20	63, 83–84		
29:32	18	17:14	87		
30:1	18	20:12	43, 75n10		
30:1–3	18	21:15	75n10		
30:14	19	21:17	75n10		
30:18–22	19	22:16	66		
30:21	62	32:6	6		
30:22	19				
31:34	103	**Leviticus**			
32:29	8	10:3	57n10		
33:5	15	12:2–5	61		
34:5	64	18:15	96		
34:13	64	19:3	43, 75n10		
34:30	64	20:9	75n10		
34:31	64				
35:18	41n27	**Numbers**			
35:19	19–20	11:12	107		
35:22	19, 20, 25n43	12:1	84		
35:27–29	15	12:15	84		
36:1–22	57n8	13:33	104n1		
37:31–34	103	20:2	84		
38	74n2, 117n20	26:58	63		
38:7–11	101				
38:14–18	102	**Deuteronomy**			
38:15	102	5:16	43, 75n10		
40–66	60	22:13	61		
42	75–76n18	22:17, 21	61		
42:13	60	22:28–29	66		
46:8, 15	65	25:1–4	117n20		

27:23	77n37	3:3		69
32	108	3:5		69
32:11ff.	108	4:1–5		70
33:6	20	4:11		25n47
34:10	83	4:12		69
		4:14–15		69
		4:15		70
Joshua	89			
2:1–24	90	**1 Samuel**		26
2:12	89	1–2		24n40
6:22–25	90	1:1–6		31, 77n31
6:25		1:8		31
		1:11		31
Judges	103	1:14–15		32
3:12–31	79, 80, 81,92	1:26–28		33
4	80	2		33
4:4, 5	80	2:5, 7		32
4:6	103	2:19		103
4:17–24	37, 80, 81, 92	19:11–17		91
5	37	28		91
8:29–9:57	37	28:15		
10:6–12:7	70			
12:34–40	40n8, 40n19	**2 Samuel**		
13	26	1–3		46–47
13–16	27	3:2		65
13:2	27	3:3		65
13:2–25	28	3:7–9		57n22
13:4	28	6:22		57n11
13:24	29	11:18–28		57n8
14:4	29	12:18		57n10
15:15	30	13		44, 65, 66
16:28	37	13:6		66
17:1	104n3	13:13		65
19	70	13:17		65
19:1–20:6	74n5	13:20		66
21:16–24		14		45
		14:1–22		44
Ruth		14:4–17		24n33
1:8	72, 75n12	14:11		45
1:8–9	68	19:1		57n10
1:16–18	68	20		45
2:19–23	68	20:16–19		93n1
2:20	76n29	20:17–22		44
3:1	68	20:19		45
3:1ff.	68			

20:22	45	**1 Chronicles**	
21:4–14	57n22	4:3	40n8
		4:9	26
1 Kings		4:9–10	35, 36
1–2	50	4:13	41n24
1:17–18	50	4:18	75n13
1:29–30	50	5:1	20
1:32–40	52		
2:13–18	51	**2 Chronicles**	
2:20–21	51	11:20	53
3:16–27	46	15:16	53
3:23–26	46	22:2–12	55
3:25	46	23:12–21	55
15:2, 10	53	24:7	55
15:30	49	34:11–28	87
16–21	54		
22:2	88	**Nehemiah**	
22:11	88	9:21	109
22:16–17	88		
22:19–20	88	**Esther**	
		1:12–22	85
2 Kings		2:2–4	85
4:8	34	2:8	85
4:8–37	34	2:9	85
4:9–38	26	2:10, 20	86
4:13	34	2:17–18	86
4:16	34	9:13	86
4:19	35	9:28	94n19
4:34–37	35	9:29f.	87
6:24–30	38	9:29–32	86
6:29	38		
6:30	38	**Psalms**	
9	54	45	52–53, 58n24
11:1	55	85:15	116n14
11:1–20	55	92:12	105n12
11:3	54–55	99:6	40n21
18:18	57n8	103:13	112, 116n15
19:21	74n5	114:4	116n14
21:1	49, 77n40		
22:14–20	87	**Proverbs**	
23:31	53	1–9	43, 44, 77n34
24:8	54	1:7	43
24:12	54	1:8	43, 75n10
24:18	53	1:20	43
25:27–30	53		

Index

4:3 77n42
6:20 43, 75n10
9:1 43
10:1 56n5
15:20 56n5
18:1 100
19:26 56n5
20:20 56n5, 75n10
23:22, 25 56n5
31 44
31:1–9 51–52
31:10 44
31:10–31 77n34
31:21ff. 109
31:28–29 44

Song of Songs
1:6 71, 72, 73
2:15 71
3 53
3:3 71
3:4 71, 75n12
3:11 51, 71, 73
4:4 73
5:7 71
6:9 71, 73
8:1 71, 72, 73
8:2 71, 75n12
8:5 71
8:8–9 71–72, 73
8:8–10 71

Isaiah
1–39 115
1:8 74n5
3:16 74n5, 110
4:1 110
5:1–7 74n5
5:7 97
15:2 74n5
32:11–12 74n5
37:22 74n5
40–55 116n10
40–66 107, 115, 116n10
42:13 110

42:14 110
46:3 111
49:15 111, 112, 113
51:2 115
54:6–7 117n20
56–66 116n10
60:15–16 117n20
62:4 77n40, 117n20
65:17 109
66:7–9 111
66:8 111
66:9 111
66:13 113
66:22 109

Jeremiah
4:31 116n9
6:24 116n9
7:29 74n5
9:3 16
9:17 74n5
13:18 54
13:21 116n9
15:1 40n21
16:6 74n5
19:9 38
22:23 116n9
29:2 54
30:5–7 109
30:6 116n9
30:15–22 113
31:14–16 22
31:14–17 21
31:15ff 25n45
31:15–17 115
31:16 25n48
41:5 74n5
47:5 74n5
48:37 74n5
48:41 116n9
49:24 116n9
50:43 116n9
51:5 75n9, 114
52:1 53
52:1–2 53–54

Lamentations
1:6, 8–9	74n5
2:20	38
4:10	38
9:3–16	103

Ezekiel
16:44–45	62
16:49–50	97

Hosea
4:4	108
11:1–11	108
12:3–4	16

Joel
2:13	116n14

Jonah
4:2	116n14

Micah
1:16	74n5
6:4	84, 115
7:6	62

Baruch
3:26–28	104

Ben Sira
7:24–25	76n24
22:3–5	76n24

Hebrews
11:31	91, 94n27

James
2:25	94n27

Jubilees
17:4	7